ENDORSEMENTS

"Dave is a longtime friend of mine who has consistently been a leading thinker on the Church of today and of tomorrow. He helps us challenge our past assumptions and current models to ensure the Church stays on the forefront of innovation."

— BOBBY GRUENEWALD,
Founder/CEO of YouVersion and
Pastor & Innovation Leader at Life.Church

"As leaders, COVID-19 gave us an opportunity to ask ourselves some big questions about our model for doing church, and how we leverage technology to reach people in our communities, and help them develop daily disciplines. These questions need to be asked, and in *MetaChurch*, Dave Adamson provides some answers based on his experience as one of the first online pastors in the world. This book will challenge you, but it will also inspire you to think beyond what you've always done in order to go into all the world and preach the Gospel."

— MARK BATTERSON,
New York Times* Best-selling Author of *The Circle Maker
and Lead Pastor of National Community Church

"I had the privilege of working with Dave for seven years. He was instrumental in the development of our social media and online strategy for our Atlanta area churches. I'm thrilled he's making the insight and knowledge he brought to our team available to yours! You will walk away from this book smarter, better equipped, and encouraged to make the most of the tremendous opportunities technology makes available to ministries of all sizes."

— ANDY STANLEY,
Bestselling Author and Founder of North Point Ministries

"In his book, *MetaChurch*, Dave Adamson makes a compelling argument that it is time we reimagine the way we do church without ever compromising the why. Discipleship has moved beyond mere attendance and entered the realm of engagement. Drawing on years of his online experience, Dave is committed to helping us dig new wells before old brooks dry up."

– LISA BEVERE,
***NYT* Best-selling Author, Co-founder of**
Messenger International & MessengerX App

"I have long appreciated Dave Adamson's voice in the Church. *MetaChurch* will both surprise you in places and shock you in others. And in it, you'll find a better path toward the future. Are Dave's ideas disruptive? Yes. And that's exactly what the Church needs. Disrupt yourself, or be disrupted."

– CAREY NIEUWHOF,
Best-selling Author, Speaker, and Host of
The Carey Nieuwhof Leadership Podcast

"Blockbuster is no longer in business because they couldn't imagine a world where people wouldn't want to get in their car and drive to a building for their products. Many churches have permanently closed their doors because they couldn't imagine a world where people wouldn't want to get in their car and drive to a building for their service. That world is not imaginary. We are living in it. And this is why *MetaChurch* is required reading for every pastor who believes we are called to make disciples . . . not attenders."

– NONA JONES,
Tech Executive, Pastor, and Best-selling Author
of *From Social Media to Social Ministry*

"When we launched North Point Online back in 2009, we weren't quite sure what we were doing. In some ways, it was an idea in search of a strategy. Now, almost every church has an online presence but the strategy is often still missing. That's why Dave's book is such a gift. It will help you connect your online presence with a sound ministry strategy."

– JEFF HENDERSON,
Founding Pastor of Gwinnett Church, and
Author of *Know What You're FOR and What to Do Next*

"We are not in a temporary season. This is a transition to a new era and Dave Adamson is holding a mirror to prompt a new paradigm. He has been an inspiration, challenge, and wonderful guide in this online season for Alpha Australia. Dave has helped us greatly, and this book will help you articulate and identify the essentials to consider. It was challenging, inspiring, painful, and truth telling for my ministry's future, and I'm becoming an advocate for *MetaChurch*."

— MELINDA DWIGHT,
National Director for Alpha Australia

"I have loved getting to know Dave through technology, which is how so many people in the future are going to get to know Jesus. We all need to take the advice in this book if we are passionate about reaching others for Christ. Dave's methods are not just theoretical, they were born out of his experience and will be helpful to anyone in ministry. Read this book and share it with others."

— JONATHAN POKLUDA,
Best-selling Author, Host of *Becoming*
***Something*, and Pastor of Harris Creek**

"Dave Adamson is an insightful leader. He has, over many years, been able to help churches navigate new technologies. More than ever, we have discovered the need for our churches to continue to innovate, in order to get the gospel message out, and to reach the world with the love of Jesus. *MetaChurch* will undoubtedly be both a challenge and an encouragement to those who read it. You may not agree with everything Dave writes. That's okay. Pioneers and prophets will always stretch our paradigms. I trust that you will find in the pages of this book, inspiration and practical help in growing digital ministry as a part of your church's mission."

— PASTOR WAYNE ALCORN,
National President of Australian Christian Churches

"Finally! We've got the practical playbook for digital discipleship that pastors have been praying for! *MetaChurch* isn't some theory about a far-off future, it's a step-by-step blueprint to architect your church's online strategy now! Dave is not just a practitioner, he's a pastor who has seen the future of digital discipleship. So if you're ready to pour the timeless Gospel through new digital wineskins, Dave provides a practical, step-by-step guide for engaging thirsty seekers online."

— **TIM LUCAS,**
Lead Pastor of Liquid Church

"If there is one church social media book I'd recommend reading this year, this would be it. *MetaChurch* not only brings up important questions, it gives practical advice for getting started and taking your church social media to the next level."

— **BEAU COFFRON,**
Life.Church Social Media Director

"In his new book, *MetaChurch*, Aussie Dave shows how churches need to keep rethinking their approach to ministry in an increasingly digital world. Dave's been at the headwaters of this new frontier long before the world had to cope with a pandemic. Just as the Apostle Paul was willing to become all things to reach people beyond the reach of the Gospel, Dave shows us the way forward. There are no simple answers and the landscape keeps changing. But we must keep pressing forward. If you're a ministry leader looking to reach an increasingly digital world, I highly recommend you read this book."

— **PHIL MERSHON,**
Director of Events and Social Media Examiner

"Dave is one of the few thought leaders around digital and the Church. I always love how he thinks and challenges every pastor to integrate digital. Can't wait to dive into his book."

— **JAY KRANDA,**
Online Community Pastor of Saddleback Church

"Dave first got my attention with his Hebrew words on social media. Since meeting him and becoming friends, we have had many conversations about *MetaChurch*. I was enthralled reading this and feel urgent for everyone to understand where we are headed but also where we have been. There is a lot to navigate as the Church moves forward and it seems the future may belong to those who can know and understand the times, and also hear what the Spirit is saying. Dave Adamson has a grasp on both, and I am excited to see how this work will influence the next few decades of Church and community engagement."

— **JOEL A'BELL,**
Convoy of Hope Regional Leader — Oceania

"*MetaChurch* is the ideal companion for churches and leaders as they seek to navigate the biggest communication shift in 500 years. Dave understands the pulse of the everyday church like few I've met—and he's one of the smartest minds in the world of church tech today."

— **BRADY SHEARER,**
Founder of Pro Church Tools and Nucleus

METACHURCH

*How to Use Digital Ministry to
Reach People and Make Disciples*

DAVE ADAMSON

MetaChurch: How to Use Digital Ministry to Reach People and Make Disciples
Published by Orange, a division of The reThink Group, Inc.
5870 Charlotte Lane, Suite 300
Cumming, GA 30040 U.S.A.

All Scripture quotations, unless otherwise noted, are taken from the Holy Bible, New
International Reader's Version®, NIrV® Copyright © 1995, 1996, 1998, 2014 by
Biblica, Inc. ™ Used by permission of Zondervan. All rights reserved worldwide. www.
Zondervan.com The "NIrV" and "New International Reader's Version" are trademarks
registered in the United States Patent and Trademark Office by Biblica, Inc.™

Scripture quotations marked "NIV" are taken from the Holy Bible, New International
Version®, NIV®. Copyright © 1973, 1978, 1984, 2011 by Biblica, Inc.™ Used by
permission of Zondervan. All rights reserved worldwide. www.Zondervan.com The
"NIV" and "New International Version" are trademarks registered in the United States
Patent and Trademark Office by Biblica. Inc.™

Other Orange products are available online and direct from the publisher at
thinkorange.org. Bulk copies are available at store.thinkorange.com.

ISBN: 978-1-63570-188-3
©2022 Dave Adamson

Author: Dave Adamson
Lead Editor: Sarah Anderson
Creative Director: Ashley Shugart
Cover Design: Ashley Shugart
Book Interior Design & Layout: Jacob Hunt
Project Management: Brian Sharp
Director of Publishing: Mike Jeffries

Printed in the United States of America
First Edition 2022
1 2 3 4 5 6 7 8 9 10
03/31/2022

Dedicated to:

Chelsea, Ella, and Jordyn

May you, your children, and your grandchildren inherit a Church that is better placed to deal with the future.

CONTENTS

METACHURCH

INTRODUCTION

"

*When used right, technology becomes an
accelerator of momentum, not a creator of it.*

JIM COLLINS, *GOOD TO GREAT: WHY SOME COMPANIES
MAKE THE LEAP AND OTHERS DON'T*

WE HAVE LIVED THROUGH A monumental moment in Church history.

In March 2020, many church leaders around the world experienced online services for the very first time. While a gaggle of tech-savvy churches (I'm pretty sure "gaggle" is the collective noun for tech-savvy churches, but if it's not, it should be) had been streaming Sunday services live online for a decade or more, the majority of church world went into full-blown scramble mode. When the COVID-19 pandemic forced churches across the planet to temporarily close their doors, there was no other option than to stream services live or post them pre-recorded to websites, Facebook, YouTube, or other online platforms.

This constituted an enormous shift in the model for church—possibly the biggest shift since the protestant Reformation in the 1500s. At the very least, it was the largest church shift any of us had experienced in our lifetimes. But COVID-19 lockdowns didn't start online church—they just forced it to go mainstream.

About 13 years before COVID-19 changed the Church, I left my career as a TV sports reporter in Melbourne, Australia and moved with my wife Meg, and three daughters—Chelsea, Ella, and Jordyn—to New Jersey. There, I joined the staff of a church called Liquid and became the 8th online pastor in the world (more about that later). And it didn't take me long to learn that church online played second-fiddle to church onsite.

By the time COVID-19 lockdowns forced thousands of church leaders around the world to hurriedly work out how to stream services online in 2020, I had been the online and social media pastor at North Point Ministries in Atlanta for six years. With every service at every church going online, this was every digital pastor's Super Bowl.

An online stream that had been the understudy to the live, in-person, physical "main" service, was now taking center stage!

But, what started out as excitement soon became stress. The "Super Bowl" took its toll—not just on me, but on online pastors around the world. Normal work days turned into 14–18 hour stretches as we helped churches around the world get their live streams up and running. It brought me to the brink of burn out, and led my doctor to prescribe antidepressants and order me to slow down.

Thankfully, by the end of August 2020, things started to improve. The calls I was having with church leaders were finally starting to shift. People had stopped asking about how to do online *streaming*, and were instead asking how to do online *ministry*.

And that subtle change in language represented a massive change in philosophy.

It seemed that many pastors were starting to realize their approach to digital technology in the church had been far too short-sighted. Online church, they were starting to see, was not just a way to broadcast their services, but it was a way to connect with people. As my friend Beau Coffron, social media director at Life.Church puts it, "Church online *is* a ministry, it doesn't just point to a ministry."

But while some pastors were beginning to see the reach and impact possibilities of online ministry, not everyone was tracking. During this time there were still many church leaders who publicly discredited online church while expressing their preference for in-person worship. For example, they'd write things like, "Internet church is not real church." Or they'd announce at conferences that, "there is no such thing as Zoom church!"[1] Or post that, "watching church from the outside is like being an observer instead of a participant" or that online service streams were "fundamentally inadequate."

DIGGING NEW WELLS

Some of the pushback to online church came from pastors who had an instinctive resistance to a different model based on technology, and certainly some came because of the political undertones that came with government-mandated building closures. But to me, the push back to church online, especially during a global pandemic, indicated there was far more going on.

The tension actually reminded me of the story of Isaac digging wells, which we find in the book of Genesis. In the story, Isaac, the son of Abraham—patriarch of the three largest monotheistic world religions— is building his wealth as a landowner in a place called Gerar, which is located in what we know as south-central Israel today. In the story, we read that Isaac "became rich, and his wealth continued to grow until he became very wealthy" (Genesis 26:13 NIV). And as his household and flocks grew, Isaac started accessing the wells he had inherited from his father Abraham. But the Philistines who lived in the land at the time became jealous of his wealth, so they "filled up all of Isaac's wells with dirt" (Genesis 26:15).

So what do ancient wells filled with dirt have to do with online ministry? Well, I think there's a parallel between what Isaac was facing and what church leaders started experiencing in early 2020. Like Isaac, the Church had been doing okay for a few generations until 2020 filled up our wells with COVID, forcing us to close them down. This meant the well we had been going to every Sunday for generations—the well that always provided for us without major issue—was no longer viable. So we had to close that well down. Many of us grew discouraged and even became resentful and angry. Some of us decided it was a sign that our specific well should stay closed, while others fought in vain to keep the well open. But some church leaders, like Isaac in the narrative, decided a closed well would not be the end of their story. It was time to dig a new well. So, they started streaming online services.

5

And just like Isaac, many of the church leaders who tried this new method discovered that these new wells became a source of debate (Genesis 26:20) and even anger (Genesis 26:21). Church leaders around the world wanted their old wells back and said the new well of church online wasn't a "real" well and would never be as good as what had been handed down to them and proven so successful in the past. These church leaders publicly expressed their frustration at the dirt in the old well, wanting to go back and deal with the dirt in their own way.

Rather than waste energy on what had disrupted the way things had been, Isaac got to work reimagining what might be.

But if you read the story in Genesis 26, it's clear that Isaac didn't focus on the closed wells. Instead, he focused on the source of water. When one well closed, he simply worked with his team to open up a new well so he could continue to tap into the source. Isaac understood there was a source that would provide for his community in the new season, and rather than waste energy on what had disrupted the way things had been, he got to work reimagining what might be. He decided to dig another well to make sure he—and the people he was leading—could access that source.

Eventually, Isaac liked the new well so much he named it, "open space," because God "created enough space for us to prosper in this land" (Genesis 26:22).

The events of 2020 and 2021 forced almost every church leader in the world to find another well.

At the same time, many of us debated the merits and validity of the new well. We got frustrated, discouraged, and maybe a little angry because of what was being asked of us in order to pivot in this new world. Yet, what if the thing we experienced as a disruption was actually an invitation? Maybe, this well called "cyberspace" could/would allow the Church to prosper in a new season. Maybe it was more than just a way to cope until things got back to "normal." Maybe this new "well" could actually serve as the catalyst for the Church of the *future* and do more for the Church than we could ever imagine.

6

Now, it's very easy for me to just write that, but let's be honest: change of any sort is hard. There's a cost to rethinking, much less re-digging new wells or models of church, that we've invested so much in over a long time. Every church leader has a model or approach or way of doing church. Changing our model requires us working through issues of theology, rethinking definitions of community, reimagining our idea of discipleship and ministry, and rewriting our long-held liturgies.

It can be overwhelming. It *will* be frustrating.

That's why my hope in writing this book is that it will energize you with fresh purpose and provide you with strategic ideas that will help you move beyond some of the frustrations that threaten to hold you back. I want the content of this book to help you rethink any preconceived ideas you may have about church online and church in-person, and to consider a world in which the two models do not compete, but compliment one another.

As you dig in, you'll notice I included some practical tips and best practices, but have intentionally steered away from multi-platform hacks, in favor of a general, overarching approach to online ministry. What I want to offer is a new methodology that works no matter what changes in the technological space. I wanted to provide a framework through which you can approach any new online platforms that come along. That's why you'll find in this book an evergreen approach to using technology in your church context, rather than a step-by-step guide to any one specific platform.

MOVING INTO DEEPER WATER

Whenever I think of church leaders wrestling with the idea of online ministry, I always remember one of my favorite places to visit in the Holy Land on the northwestern shore of the Sea of Galilee. This is the place where it's believed Jesus once asked a group of fishermen to "put out into the deep and let down your nets for a catch" (Luke 5:4). We usually don't even think about this request, because we're focused on the end result—the fishermen pulling in a miraculous haul of fish. But this initial request Jesus made is worth paying attention to.

The Hebrew word we translate as "deep water" throughout the Bible is "tehom" (תהום pronounced 'teh-home'), which often refers to chaos and confusion. This is the word used in the creation story in Genesis, when God brings light to the darkness, the flood story when God restrains the chaos of the deep water, and the Exodus story when God parts the Red Sea so the Hebrews can get safely through the deep water.

In this story found in Luke, Jesus asked His followers to move out into deep water—to step *into* chaos, confusion, and disorder. And when they chose to trust Jesus, the result was a miracle—so many fish that the boats were in danger of capsizing. By trusting Jesus in the middle of their chaos, they got more than they could ever have imagined! There is SO much more to this story, but that's for another day and another book.

Church leaders around the world experienced "tehom" in the first quarter of 2020. For some of you, the chaos and disorder of that season piled on what was already a difficult situation. That's why I want to encourage all of us to remember that when the disciples did what Jesus asked, when they tried something new and "put out into the deep," something unexpected happened. I'm not saying your church will increase in number ten fold if you try this new approach to ministry. But I am saying that it's possible you're missing out on something by *not* trying something new.

My hope and prayer for you as you read this book, is that you will approach what feels like chaos with expectation, believing that as you focus on the source of living water, instead of the well you've always used, you will see God do something you don't expect. It may not be that you catch such a large number of fish that your Internet will break—God may just want to do something unexpected in you.

This hope is rooted in wanting to help local pastors from my years of experience in this space, partly because I want to serve the capital C church. But, if I'm honest, mostly I do this because I'm a dad. My three daughters, Chelsea, Ella, and Jordyn, have grown up as digital natives, so they've made major life discoveries and decisions online. This is their reality. And because of that, I simply want to make sure my kids and yours, the ones who have already entered our buildings and those who may never come through our physical doors, inherit a Church that is better equipped and more strategically placed to deal with the future that is right around the corner.

1

**PHILOSOPHICAL
ARGUMENT**

CHAPTER 01

SMART LIGHTS AND ANALOGUE BASKETS

"

The Church always seems to be behind the times, when it is really beyond the times.

G. K. CHESTERTON

IF COVID-19 HAD HIT IN 1989 when I was in high school, I would have been screwed.

My fellow Gen-Xers and I would not have had an option for online learning or live-streamed classes—we would have simply lost a year or so of school and most likely had to repeat the grade we were in. And it's not like we could have spent our days watching movies, because streaming entertainment wasn't a thing, all the cinemas would have closed their doors, and the local Blockbuster or family video store would have been off-limits. The movies our family had on VHS would have been the only options available to us.

But that's just the beginning. When hard lockdowns were inevitably introduced, there would have been no way for us to get groceries delivered to our house because online shopping was a distant dream, Amazon hadn't been invented yet, and UberEats was decades away.

And since video calls, group chats, Dropbox, Slack, Airdrop, and file sharing were the stuff of science fiction back in 1989, it's not like anyone would have been able to work from home effectively—even if they were in an industry that didn't require them to be physically present. In other words, a worldwide pandemic that closed down offices and factory floors would have taken an even bigger toll on the economy in 1989 than it did in 2020.

Now, obviously, we all wish there had never been a pandemic—no matter what the year. Like you, COVID changed my world. As a pastor, I've seen the emotional toll COVID has taken on friends who have lost loved ones, the financial toll it's taken on those who have lost work, and witnessed the physical impact it has had on close friends who were hospitalized with the virus. As a dad, I've also experienced the mental toll COVID has had on my daughters who were forced into virtual learning for an entire school year and separated from friends. And, I had firsthand experience with the depression, stress, and anxiety the pandemic created for so many of us.

But if it's possible to say there was a silver lining to the pandemic, I would say it was this: we had a technological infrastructure that allowed for some semblance of normalcy. From simple things like being able to shop for groceries online and having them delivered, to being able to have video consultations with our doctor, digital technology allowed life, in many ways, to go on.

Zoom made it possible for my wife and I to stay connected with our work and ministry colleagues. Online learning kept my daughters up-to-date with their education. Amazon Prime meant we could still have everything we needed delivered to our front door. And Netflix, Disney+, and AppleTV kept us all entertained/sane.

In many ways, the COVID-19 pandemic proved just how much of our lives had already moved online.

This became increasingly obvious when the organizations that had already embraced online and digital technology *before* the pandemic, thrived *during* the pandemic. According to a New York Times[2] report in April 2021, Amazon's profits soared after March 2020. Even into the first quarter of 2021, the multinational e-commerce giant was still seeing 220% increases in its bottom line. Likewise, Netflix added 16 million subscribers in the first quarter of 2020 according to Forbes[3]— the largest three month jump in the company's history.

And it wasn't just large tech companies that flourished. The Wall Street Journal[4] reported that online marketplace Etsy doubled its revenue in 2020, while online delivery services like Uber Eats, GrubHub, and Doordash also experienced huge growth[5].

And, of course, Zoom—a company most of us had never even heard of prior to 2020—saw its profits quadruple in 2020, with an additional 40% increase expected in 2021, at the time of this writing. In January 2020, shares for the video conferencing platform were selling for just over $76, but by October of that same year, they were going for $559 per share. That is a 635% increase!

In large part, these companies succeeded because long before the pandemic, they were already taking full advantage of online and digital technology.

> **And yet, despite watching these organizations meet real needs in tangible ways and grow in the process, we have been hesitant to believe in the value of a specific online model.**

All of these organizations had well-established models built for a world that had been increasingly moving online for years. Their penchant for innovating new, convenient experiences for their customers allowed them to be perfectly positioned when COVID lockdowns started crippling their brick-and-mortar competitors. Many of these organizations were so well-established that their company names had become verbs in our modern vernacular long before March 2020. Date nights had become a time to "Netflix and chill." We didn't just shop online anymore, we, "Amazon Primed." And how many times have we answered the daily "what's for dinner?" question with "I'm just gonna UberEats something"?!

We would be hard pressed to find a person in the western world who didn't benefit from the online infrastructure these companies had established. And yet, despite watching these organizations meet real needs in tangible ways and grow in the process, we have been hesitant to believe in the value of a specific online model. Pre-COVID, many pastors and ministry leaders gave online teams the scraps of church resources—if any— and treated online services as little more than a by-product of the "main" event. Even at churches that had long-established online services, pastors openly encouraged their online community to get serious about their church by attending physically.

THE APOSTLE PAUL
AND ONLINE CHURCH

While our own lives moved increasingly online before the pandemic—using Peleton to stay fit, podcasts to stay educated, and audiobooks to stay well-read—we still insisted that people get in their cars and drive to our buildings on Sunday mornings to attend our churches physically, in order for it to "count." So when the world shut down with the COVID outbreak, the technological chasm between the Church and the rest of the world became blatantly obvious. That's when a lot of us realized, "but that's the way we've always done it" is not a good enough reason for the Church to avoid innovating and updating its model.

We all probably agree with Craig Groeschel, Senior Pastor of Life. Church, who has said many times, "To reach people no one is reaching, we have to do things no one is doing" . . . right up to the point where we actually have to start doing the thing no one is doing.

The irony is, even the in-person church model most of us follow today flies in the face of the Apostle Paul, the most well known New Testament writer. Paul was rarely "in person" to meet with the church communities he started and pastored. He relied heavily on the technology of his day to teach them, encourage them, and stay connected with them. The technology of Paul's day was letter writing. (For those of you under the age of 30, letter writing is when you have a piece of paper, you push a pen down onto it, and then move your wrist around to form letters! This is how Paul discipled his community when he was forced to be socially distant from them.)

Social media is the technology of the day: podcasts, video-on-demand, live streaming, and YouTube. Yet, instead of leveraging this technology in the same way Paul did—to connect people with each other and with God—we've decided the only way to properly lead, teach, and disciple people, is through face-to-face, in-person, physical services.

But if Paul had thought like many modern-day pastors—that the *only* way he could teach and disciple people was in physical, face-to-face community—at least 13 of the 27 books of the New Testament would not have been written. Fortunately for us, Paul embraced the technology of his day and used it to expand his reach beyond his physical location. Perhaps it was because he recalled that when the Church started, "the believers devoted themselves to the apostles' teaching" (Acts 2:42) and not a specific *model* of teaching, so he felt confident using technology to teach people.

The problem is, it seems the Church has lost Paul's innovative and creative spirit. Could it be that the community that Jesus said would be "... the light of the world" (Matthew 5:14) has willingly decided to hide its light under an analogue basket for the sake of tradition? Even as we move forward from those first years impacted by COVID, church leaders continue to question the legitimacy of online church, ignoring the fact that every single day, people carry a pulpit, worship team, small group, and an offering plate in their pockets in the form of their phones.

> **In a world of smartphones, smart homes, smartwatches, smart lights and smart cars, the Church has found itself outsmarted.**

In a world of smartphones, smart homes, smartwatches, smart lights, and smart cars, the Church has found itself outsmarted. Somewhere along the way, we got in our minds that tradition was worth protecting at all costs—even at the expense of effectiveness. We convinced ourselves that technology and innovation were the enemies of the Church, so if a new technology came out, it meant it must be wrong. And since we have a tendency to make culture the enemy of the Church, if culture adopted a new technology and was using it well, we clutched our collective pearls and declared that must be wrong too!

We experienced in real time the problem with this way of thinking in 2020, when the world changed and the Church wasn't ready. And so, the Church was exposed as an offline organization struggling to survive in an online world—not because we didn't have access to the same technology as everyone else, but because we made a conscious decision *not* to change for the sake of tradition.

But the Gospel deserves better than that.

Models of doing church aren't issues of right and wrong; they are a question of being *effective* or *ineffective*. If we remain unwilling to reconsider our approach to church, people will do it for us. This is why we can't afford to lag behind technologically just because learning something new discomforts us.

And so, my hope is, the ideas and strategies laid out in the pages that follow, provide a place for you to start a new era for your church—an era that challenges the traditionally held norms, but is willing to get uncomfortable for the sake of reaching the people in this new world we live in.

CHAPTER 02

THE CASE FOR ONLINE CHURCH

"

The Church has opposed every innovation and discovery from the day of Galileo down to our own time, when the use of anesthetics in childbirth was regarded as a sin because it avoided the biblical curse pronounced against Eve.

MARK TWAIN

LIKE MOST PASTORS, I'VE PERFORMED many weddings. And, like most pastors, the couples I've married hold a special place in my heart. I guess I feel more responsible for those couples since I was the one who made their marriage legal.

That's why I answered the call I got late one Friday night, from a guy whose wedding I had officiated five years earlier.

"Pastor Dave! Could you please talk to my wife?" The concern coming from the voice on the other end of the line was hard to miss.

"Sure . . . what's going on?" I asked.

"Well, she's upset with me."

The upset husband then went on to explain that his wife had found some direct messages on his phone from a social media platform,

19

in which he had been communicating with a woman who was not his wife. "She's accusing me of flirting with another woman!" he cried.

Before I had a chance to ask any more questions, he put the phone on speaker mode and his clearly emotional wife spoke up. "I feel so betrayed. I don't know what to think," she said.

In an effort to get to the bottom of the situation, I started to ask some clarifying questions. And as I did, it became obvious there was plenty to be concerned about. Based on the content of the messages that were being read out loud to me, it was obvious the husband had been flirting with a woman online, and was upset he had been caught. When I stated as much, the exasperated husband blurted, "How can it be flirting? I've never even met this woman! It's all online so it's not even real. There's nothing to worry about."

> **In the same way that the negatives of flirting and bullying online can significantly impact people and relationships, worshiping God online can have an equally positive impact.**

I don't need to tell you how that defense went over with his wife. The fact that this interaction happened online didn't make it less real—to his wife or to me as a third party observer. In fact, I'm sure that everyone reading this would agree that online flirting presents as real an issue for a marriage as in-person flirting. It would be difficult to make an opposing case!

And yet, there are many church leaders who applied the same logic to church online, arguing that watching live-streamed services, or participating in church online "doesn't count" because it's not in-person. Just like the wife whose husband is flirting online, these interactions aren't any less significant because they're happening in a digital environment. Online does not mean less real. And this isn't just true with romantic relationships. Consider the impact of online bullying on students and their families.

According to U.S.-based Cyberbullying Research Center[6]:
- 36.5% of kids aged between 12 and 17 have had a bully target them online at least once in their lifetime.
- 68% of children that have gone through online harassment have experienced mental health issues.
- Victims of cyberbullying are 1.9 times more likely to commit suicide.

Try telling a student who is being bullied online—or their parents—that digital interactions aren't "real." The evidence is clear that the interactions we have online can have a profound impact on us emotionally, physically, and mentally.

And what we do online can impact us spiritually too.

In the same way that the negatives of flirting and bullying online can significantly impact people and relationships, worshiping God online can have an equally positive impact. If we agree that we can flirt and bully online, can't we worship God and build Christian community online too?

Maybe this idea makes sense to you, but there's still something about it that just doesn't *feel* right. I get it. So, let's take a closer look at the theological opposition to online church.

SOME ASSEMBLY REQUIRED!

While I've heard all sorts of arguments about the validity of online church, most seem to boil down to the definition of one word—and no, that word is NOT "ekklésia" (ἐκκλησία, pronounced "ek-klay-see'-ah" [Strong's 1577])—the word we typically translate in the Christian Bible as "assembly," "congregation," or simply "church." The word I'm referring to is "episunagógé" (ἐπισυναγωγὴν, pronounced "ep-ee-soon-ag-o-gay" [Strong's 1997]) which is translated as "assembling together" in Hebrews 10:25.

"And let us not neglect our meeting together, as some people do, but encourage one another, especially now that the day of his return is drawing near." (NLT)

"Not forsaking the assembling of ourselves together, as the manner of some is; but exhorting one another: and so much the more, as ye see the day approaching." (KJV)

". . . not neglecting to meet together, as is the habit of some, but encouraging one another, and all the more as you see the Day drawing near." (ESV)

This verse, more than any other, is the one church online advocates hear regularly coming from those suspicious of the legitimacy of digital ministry.

The anti-church-online argument usually starts with some variation of, "church online is not valid because we're told to not give up meeting together . . ." After years of hearing this argument, I want to concede that this verse is definitely referring to physical gatherings. But this doesn't mean "meeting together" was ONLY referring to physical gatherings. In the first century, there was no such thing as Zoom, FaceTime, or video conferencing, so there was no other option but to gather physically. In other words, to give up meeting together in person then, was to give up meeting together, period. But that simply isn't the case for us. To suggest this verse mandates physical gathering is to limit the Scriptures.

It would be the same as a pastor suggesting a digital version of the Bible is not the actual Bible, because when the authors of the Bible make mention of the Scriptures (2 Timothy 3:16 for example), they were referring to the Torah scrolls of their day that were made from parchment or animal skins. But I've never heard a pastor argue that the Bible app or an online Bible didn't "count" or wasn't "real."

Or, would a pastor ever suggest that the verse that asks believers to, "Bring the whole tithe into the storehouse . . ." (Malachi 3:10) means the Church should only accept cash brought physically to a church building? No! Most churches these days are happy to accept any form of giving, including: electronic bank transfers, Venmo, Cash App, Beamit, Pushpay, Tithely, and more. I've even been to a church in Australia that accepted stocks and cryptocurrency as offerings. I've never heard anyone suggest online giving in church is "not real" because when technology changed the way we manage our finances, the Church adjusted accordingly.

In the same way, the Church needs to rethink its definition of "gather together" or "assemble together." That doesn't mean we should throw the old definition of "episunagógé" away altogether, but rather, we need to expand and broaden the interpretation. The writer of Hebrews tells us that "the word of God is alive and active," which means it doesn't remain flat or stagnant and neither does its application. God's word is supposed to move in and out of cultural contexts and it should be practical in every application. In fact, the

> **In other words, how many footsteps does a person have to take inside a church building before we are "okay" with their spiritual growth?**

original Greek word used for active in this "verse" is "ἐνεργής" which means "effective"—it's effective at achieving God's desired results. We need to ensure the definition of "gather together" is effective for today's cultural and technological moment.

This is a process the business world has been able to navigate as multinational companies have leaned into teleconferencing since the 80s, and Zoom meetings during the COVID pandemic. Likewise, the medical field has moved from house calls to in-office appointments, and now to telehealth video consultations.

So the question church leaders must work through is: Are we SO married to our model of church (buildings, pews, parking lots, stages, offices, and pulpits) that we're hesitant to innovate?

As church leaders, are we SO set in our ways that we are prepared to throw out the online church baby with the innovation bathwater?

If a friend or family member told you they had decided to stop attending their church, I'm sure most people reading these words would reach out to them to encourage them to change their mind. But what if that same person said they were not attending a physical church building, but were watching their pastor's message via live stream every Sunday, meeting in-person with their local small group during the week, giving financially to their local church via an app or an online bank transfer, and were serving a local charity in the community? Would we be concerned?

In other words, how many footsteps does a person have to take inside a church building before we are "okay" with their spiritual growth?

And that's just taking into consideration the people for whom attending is relatively easy. What about the nurse who works the graveyard emergency shift every Saturday night and is sleeping in on Sunday in order to pull another shift Sunday evening? Or the small business owner who has to stay open all weekend to be able to pay their employees and put food on their own table? Or the student with extreme social anxiety? Or the families with shared custody of children with special needs? Or countless other complexities people face?

Without meaning to, many church leaders may be establishing arbitrary guidelines for who gets a "pass" for missing church and who doesn't—all in the name of in-person community.

While some could argue that people who watch online church services are not fully embracing community, wouldn't that also be true of those who attend a brick and mortar church every Sunday yet arrive after worship and leave before the message is over to avoid people?

The point is, if Christianity is going to remain an effective force in an ever changing culture, we need to believe that online church is a viable aspect of the modern Church.

ENHANCED CHURCH

As much as I believe in online church, before we go any further, you need to hear me say this: online church should not *replace* physical church. Remember how we talked about doctor's appointments going virtual? While online consultations are advantageous in many situations, they can't replace *every* trip to the doctor. If you need a tooth extracted, your blood taken, or surgery, these procedures need to be done in-person. In the same way, there are times when certain spiritual practices and disciplines are best done in-person.

While communion can physically be conducted online via Zoom or other video conferencing for example, there's an argument to suggest that baptism requires someone else to be physically present. On the other hand, singing worship can definitely be done online, but it can be a much more powerful experience in-person. And while the post-modern world has given us a variety of new ways to gather together face-to-face digitally, staying connected physically, in-person is still extremely important.

So keep in mind, I do not believe online church could or should replace attending a brick-and-mortar, physical church building. Ever. But, I do believe online technology can be—and should be—a tool to enhance the physical church. At the most base-level, it can help church-goers who are sick or traveling for work stay connected to their church, but it can do so much more. Leveraged properly, it can help introduce and connect the local community to your church, it can be used to partner with parents to help them to teach their kids and teenagers about faith, and it can be a key component of your church's discipleship strategy.

> **Online technology can be—and should be—a tool to enhance the physical church.**

Not every church needs to stream their Sunday services—but every church should leverage some sort of digital communication to stay connected to people outside of Sunday services.

The bottom line is, Jesus stopped at nothing to meet with us. He gave up his position in time and space to fulfill God's mission of redemption. So, if we're not prepared to move from our church building space and service times to fulfill Jesus' mission of going into the world, then perhaps we've gotten it all wrong.

And we can't afford to get it wrong.

CHAPTER 03

THE ONLINE LANDSCAPE

"

While Christians may gather corporately in a sacred space that we might call a sanctuary or even a temple, the New Testament says that the church is itself a temple, a place where God dwells. This move desacralizes geographical or builtspace and elevates the mystical presence of God's Spirit in God's people.

DAVID P. GUSHEE, *AFTER EVANGELICALISM:
THE PATH TO A NEW CHRISTIANITY*

FROM MY VERY FIRST DAY as an online pastor in May 2008, church leaders, ministry experts, pastors, and basically any Christian who had thoughts on the matter, told me some variation of the opinion that church online "doesn't count" as "real" church.

"Online connections are not real connections."
"You know that's not 'real church', right?"
"Community only happens in-person!"
"Online will never be personal."
"Online church will never replace physical church!"

Back in those days, just a few years away from dial-up Internet, I totally understood where these arguments came from. Even today, I still COMPLETELY agree with the last one—church online **won't** replace in-person church! In fact, I've never met an online pastor who believes church online should, or could, replace in-person church. Every online pastor I know—myself included—sees church online as a way to enhance physical church, not replace it!

But despite this fact, criticism of any form of church online has endured, and it still comes thick and fast from pastors, speakers, preachers, and other church leaders who want to see full parking lots and full pews on Sundays. We may express it in our belief that more authentic worship happens in person or real community only takes place when we share a physical space, but I suspect there is more to it than that. Perhaps our real aversion to online church comes from the blow it gives our ego.

Too many of us in ministry measure our success and determine our self worth based on how many people are in the room listening when we preach, teach, do an altar call, or sing.

Too many of us in ministry measure our success and determine our self worth based on how many people are in the room listening when we preach, teach, do an altar call, or sing. We like knowing the numbers, we like seeing the faces, and if we are totally honest, we like the buzz it gives us to be able to draw a crowd to a specific time and place (and I can say that because I get it. I've felt the same draw). Then we justify these feelings by quoting the same verse I unpacked in the last chapter:

> *"And let us not neglect our meeting together, as some people do, but encourage one another, especially now that the day of his return is drawing near."*
> HEBREW 10:25 NLT

Again, for the sake of clarity, I'll repeat what I've said earlier. I am NOT saying that services streamed online should EVER replace in-person services. I am NOT advocating that we abandon our church buildings. However, I AM saying that online and digital technology such as social media platforms, live-streaming services, YouTube, podcasts, and apps can enhance and supplement what happens in a physical church building.

This isn't a zero sum game. We don't have to choose one model and abandon the other. We need to learn to integrate and marry the two in a way that elevates the message in the best way possible. Unfortunately, based on all the research, studies, and data I've seen from various sources, just convincing church leaders of the need to have a viable online presence isn't the only problem. In the postmodern world, the Church needs online and digital help more than ever before.

But first, let me back up.

DECENTRALIZED ATTENDANCE

The Church's physical attendance problem did not start in 2020. The data overwhelmingly shows that physical attendance in churches around the world had plateaued or was in decline long before COVID-19 closed church buildings—and people were, more than ever, accessing church content digitally.

In 2019, Pew Research[7] showed that in the U.S.:
- Only 32% of Gen X Christians attended church services every week.
- Only 22% of Millennial Christians attended weekly.

In the same year, Barna research[8] indicated:
- Only 29% of Americans of any age group who identified as church attenders, attended church weekly.

And in 2021, Statista[9] produced a report showing that:
- Only 24% of religious people attended church weekly.

Even people who attend church have stopped attending church!

But before you get too depressed, consider this: Barna also showed[10] that at the end of 2019:
- 38% of "practicing Christians" used social media to grow their faith.
- 26% accessed a sermon or message via podcast.
- 26% watched or listened to a streamed church service.

In addition to this, I know from personal experience as the online and social media pastor at North Point Ministries in Atlanta from 2013 to 2020 that, from the second half of 2018, the number of people watching messages on our church YouTube channels was exponentially increasing.

I realized long before COVID, church attendance was not decreasing, it was decentralizing.

Yet despite all this data, in February 2020, just a month before the COVID-19 pandemic impacted every local church in the world, the Barna Research Institute[11] released a "state of the church"[12] report that listed the 22 things pastors in the U.S. were most concerned about.

Church attendance was not decreasing, it was decentralizing.

Now, remember, this was February 2020, so international travel was still a thing, there were no online feuds about vaccines, drive-thru was something you only did when you were hungry, and there was still plenty of toilet paper on the shelves of every supermarket!

Back then, in that blissful pre-COVID utopia, the number one thing pastors in the U.S. were worried about was "watered down gospel teaching." Seventy-four percent of pastors were concerned about people preaching a gospel message where no one was saved. Fair enough too! We *should* care about the integrity of the message we're preaching—and given that we had no idea of what was about to happen to the world, this seems like a reasonable thing to take precedence. From there, the list included things like:

- how to reach a younger audience (6)
- church leader burnout (10)
- women in leadership (18).

And, right at the bottom of the list, at number 22, the very last thing pastors were concerned about was, "keeping up with the latest digital and technological trends."

In other words, of all the things people in full time ministry were worried about in February 2020, understanding how to leverage live streaming services, social media, YouTube, and online technology to connect with people, was at the very bottom.

I remember reading that survey in February 2020 and feeling like a failure. I had been an online pastor for 12 years when this list came out, and I was—and still am—extremely passionate about helping churches, ministries, and Christian organizations use online technology to disciple their church and engage with people in their local community.

But despite my best efforts, improvements in online and digital technology and even a COVID-enforced lockdown of church buildings, the Church is still mostly vaccinated against church online.

And if I'm honest, a part of me gets it.

CHURCH NEXT TO A PORN STORE

For a lot of us, our hesitancy to really engage in the online world for the sake of our churches has less to do with theology and tradition and more to do with outright disgust with what the Internet has become. After all, it doesn't take an online pastor to tell you that there's a lot of trash online—and it's having a negative effect on all of us. Take social media for example—the lowest hanging fruit for churches and their online presence.

In September 2021, journalists from the Wall Street Journal[13] got their hands on some internal memos from Meta (previously called Facebook) that went on to generate headlines[14] around the world[15]. The documents revealed that the social media giant is aware it's flagship product, Instagram, is toxic for the mental health of teens. The WSJ exposé[16] showed that Facebook employees are well aware that a significant percentage of young girls are negatively affected by what they see on the platform.

In fact, Facebook had conducted its own studies that showed[17]:

- 32% of teen girls said that when they felt bad about their bodies, Instagram made them feel worse.

- 6% of American users who reported suicidal thoughts traced those desires to Instagram. For British users, it was 13%.
- +178%: Suicide deaths for children ages 10 to 14 nearly tripled from 2007 to 2017, when social media saw mass adoption.

This concerned me as a pastor—and it scared the bejesus out of me as a dad to three daughters.

But that's not even the half of it. You just need to scratch the surface of statistics about online pornography to see how bad the online landscape has become.

According to porn accountability software company, Covenant Eyes[18], 28,258 people are watching pornography every second! That means in the 16 seconds it takes you to read this paragraph half a million people will have looked at pornography online. And according to data from the SEMrush Traffic Analytics[19] tool, as of May 2021, porn sites received more website traffic in the U.S. than Twitter, Instagram, Netflix, Pinterest, and LinkedIn combined, while The Guardian[20] has revealed that half of all adults in the UK watched porn during lockdowns.

So, yes, much of what can be found online is complete trash.

But that doesn't mean we should quit the Internet altogether. I think it means the exact opposite. We need churches that are light in the darkness of the online world.

In fact, when I first became an online pastor at a church called Liquid in New Jersey, I remember lead pastor, Tim Lucas, telling me in my first month on the job that by starting an online campus, I was essentially "opening a church next to a porn store." He was right. But isn't that the best place to open a church? Shouldn't the church be right there in the places where people are searching for hope and meaning?

After all, this was how Jesus himself lived, by rubbing shoulders with the outcasts of society so often that he was considered a friend of sinners—something that must be true since Casting Crowns wrote a song about it! It was such a hallmark of his ministry that the religious elite referred to him as someone who "receives sinners and eats with them" (Luke 15:2). This same group even tried to insult Jesus saying he spent so much time with the wrong people that he too was a "glutton and a drunkard, a friend of tax collectors and sinners!" (Luke 7:34).

In other words, Jesus didn't choose to steer clear of certain places simply because there was unsavory activity going on, and the modern day Church shouldn't either. Jesus went to those places and became a regular with these crowds (to the point of being mistaken for one of them!) to teach the people there about a God who wanted to connect with them. And isn't *that* what we're trying to do when we stream our services online?

As Church Leaders, we can't say we want to be like Jesus if we aren't willing to follow his example by going to the places where the people who need God the most are spending most of their time. And in the postmodern world, that's online.

The alternative is to be seen as a modern day Pharisee who waves a disapproving finger at churches that leverage online technology, or concede that while we *say* God can redeem anything, what we really mean is everything except the Internet. As Craig Groeschel once pointed out[21], Jesus didn't say: "Hey, share the Gospel everywhere. But don't share it online." But if we act like this is true, we are missing a huge opportunity, because there are a LOT of people online.

WHERE PEOPLE SPEND THEIR TIME

Research released by software developer DOMO showed that the number of people who accessed the Internet between January and July 2021, jumped by 10%, with 5.17 billion people, or 65% of the world's population, logging on.

DOMO also showed that during this period:

- Zoom hosted 856 minutes of webinars every minute.
- Netflix's 117 million subscribers streamed 140 million hours of content every day.

Meanwhile, over on YouTube, livestreams increased by 45%, with users watching 694,444 hours of video each minute for the first half of 2021. That's not a typo! 694,444 hours of video were viewed on YouTube every minute!

DOMO's research underlined the impact of online shopping too, with more than 6 million people shopping online in any given minute of the day, most of who made up the $283,000 spent on Amazon per minute. Again, not a typo!

And this is all happening at a time when, according to a Pew world-wide[22] research study in 2018, adults under 40 are less likely to be religiously affiliated. Pew found that people under 40 in the U.S., Europe, Australia, the UK, Canada, and South America were more likely to choose "atheist," "agnostic," or "nothing in particular" when asked about their religious affiliation.

Which brings me back to the Church. There are a plethora of reasons why we should avoid the pitfalls of the online world, but there's one reason why we shouldn't: *this is where people are spending most of their time.* Online is the place where we have the chance to actually be light in the world. We should do whatever we can to make it as easy as possible for people to find the front door of the Church, especially at a time when they need it most!

Right?

So, if that's what we believe, that leads us to this question: Why are so many pastors and Church Leaders wary of incorporating online and digital technology into their church model? It's a good question. And we'll tackle it next.

CHAPTER 04

WHAT ARE WE AFRAID OF?

"

Sometimes the greatest opposition to what God wants to do next, comes from those who were on the cutting edge of what God did last.

R.T. KENDALL, *THE ANOINTING*

FRANK BLAKE DOESN'T LOOK LIKE an online influencer.

He's not cut from the same cloth as Gary Vaynerchuk, Shane Dawson, PewDiePie, Kylie Jenner, Peter McKinnon, Zendaya, or Mr. Beast . . . but I consider him to be one of the foremost online influencers and digital pioneers in the Church space.

Frank was CEO of Home Depot, the largest home improvement chain in the world, from 2007 to 2015, stepping into his role at Home Depot—a top Fortune 500 company with over 2,200 retail stores—at a time when the organization was opening about 200 stores a year. But despite having a successful and proven growth strategy through the development of more physical locations, one of Frank's first moves as CEO was to stop opening new stores. You read that right—he stopped opening new physical retail stores! Instead, Frank wanted Home Depot to put its time and resources into doubling down on online retail. Rather than being a physical store only, Frank wanted Home Depot to transition into an omnichannel company, a model of shopping and customer service that would eventually put them ahead of the game.

Omnichannel is a cross-channel retail strategy that includes traditional and digital channels. It focuses on leveraging the best parts of both physical and online shopping experiences.

I once heard Frank describe the fear many Home Depot C-suite executives expressed during the early stages of the company adopting an omnichannel model: An expected drop in revenue caused by a reduction in the number of customers entering a physical store location.

Frank told me he upset a lot of people in the organization when he suggested investing heavily into online. "I had a lot of fights with people who I admire and respect, who were highly distressed at the possibility of going all-in with online. Some people thought digital retail would be a threat to the organization because it would make all of our physical assets redundant, but what we found was that when we went online, more people came to us off-line because we were more effective at meeting the customers' needs than ever before."

> **Omnichannel is a cross-channel retail strategy that includes traditional and digital channels. It focuses on leveraging the best parts of both physical and online shopping experiences.**

Frank explained to me that many of his Home Depot colleagues expressed concern. They thought if more customers opted for online shopping, less people would enter the brick-and-mortar stores, leading to reduced profits at physical locations, and the possible need to layoff in-store Home Depot associates. It all sounded familiar.

The main fear I hear from church leaders when it comes to online church is the fear of a drop in attendance. This fear is based on the assumption that streaming services online will lead to fewer people attending physical services on Sundays. People expressing this fear typically don't have any hard evidence to support this, except for the general decline in church attendance. But, long before COVID-19 forced church leaders to stream their services, church online was the patsy for decreasing church attendance.

Gallup research[23] released in March 2021 showed that church membership in the U.S. had been in sharp decline, long before COVID, since the turn of the 21st century:

- In 1999, 70% of Americans said they were members of a church.
- In 2000, 69% identified as members of a church.
- In 2008, 62% identified as members of a church.
- In 2016, 52% identified as members of a church.
- In 2018, 50% identified as members of a church.
- In 2021, 47% of U.S. adults identified as members of a church.

This 2021 figure was the first time the number had dropped below 50% since Gallup first started measuring church membership in 1937.

Because a decline in church attendance was a thing long before the creation of the Internet, believing that online church is the cause of this attendance drop is to oversimplify a complex problem. According to Gallup senior editor[24], Jeffrey M. Jones, Ph.D., the decline has been due to an increase in lack of religious affiliation. "The decline in church membership is primarily a function of the increasing number of Americans who express no religious preference," Jones writes. "Over the past two decades, the percentage of Americans who do not identify with any religion has grown from 8% in 1998-2000 to 13% in 2008-2010 and 21% over the past three years."

Simply put: church online is not to blame for the decrease in church attendance.

This is where Frank Blake and Home Depot's omnichannel approach comes to the rescue, and why I think Frank is an online pioneer. From the moment I heard of Frank's strategy for HomeDepot.com, I've believed this answered the FIDA (fear in dropping attendance) plaguing the church.

Faced with growing concerns about the future of brick-and-mortar stores if HomeDepot.com became too popular with customers, Frank and his team *linked the online store with the physical store.* They established a click and collect option which would allow customers to make a purchase online, but rather than wait 5-days for delivery, they could pick up their item in-person the same day. This gave them an advantage that their digital rival, Amazon, could not compete with. Along with a physical pick-up option, Home Depot also allowed customers the convenience of returning online orders in-person if needed.

This was the foundation of Home Depot's omnichannel approach—online and in-person working *together* for a seamless shopping experience.

"There were a lot of people at Home Depot who thought the Internet was a threat to us as an organization, but it wasn't a threat at all to our customers," Frank told me. "They loved it. To them it was a very efficient modality. And I think it's the same in the church. Too often church leaders see online as a threat to their organizations, but the people who attend our churches love it!"

While many customers took fewer footsteps into their local Home Depot store, they spent more money thanks to the digital and physical options available. By 2017, 43% of Home Depot's online orders[25] were collected in store and over 90% were returned in store. Digital and physical stores work together in a mutually beneficial, symbiotic relationship with each driving deeper connection with the other.

Frank told me that he believed the same thing could happen in churches, with digital technology amplifying the mission. Frank said, "I remember hearing Andy [Stanley] say one day that most organizations start by providing great answers to people's problems, but when they grow to a certain size, they become focused on being a great answer to their own problems. A lot of churches still see digital as a threat that they need to manage but it can make your mission enormously effective because it allows you to help people in your community. I think many faith communities think of the Internet as a broadcast model, but it's not. The Internet is the opposite of a broadcast model because it is a narrow-cast model that allows you to have one-on-one engagement and interactions with people."

Simply put: church online is not to blame for decreasing church attendance.

Craig Menear, the new Home Depot president and CEO, told Forbes Magazine[26] in February 2020 that shopping at Home Depot was a fully interconnected physical and digital experience. And he added that online shopping had led to more people visiting physical locations. "HomeDepot.com continues to be an engine for growth[27] of our overall business, driving increased traffic online and additional footsteps to our stores," Menear said. "This is the power of the interconnected retail strategy."

FEAR OF INNOVATION

Online activity drives more in-person visits. This is true in the business of shopping, and I believe it can be true in the Church. But for this to become reality, church leaders need to get over the Fear of Innovation.

In his New York Times bestselling book *Originals: How Non-Conformists Move The World*, organizational psychologist Adam Grant notes that when our "achievement motivation goes sky-high, it can crowd out originality. The more you value achievement, the more you come to dread failure. Instead of aiming for unique accomplishments, the intense desire to succeed leads us to strive for guaranteed success."

So what does that have to do with church?

When a church leader achieves their attendance, building, staffing, or small group goal, they tend to start playing things safe. When they taste the "success" that comes from large crowds and large resources, Grant would argue that the innovation that got them to that goal stops, because they're more inclined to stick with what's safe. As a result, doing the things that worked for the church in the past is the approach for the church's future. When there is a lack of success, the motivation for innovation is high—but the fear of failure *after* success brings with it a fear of innovation.

The exercise of innovation requires a risk, sacrifice, and commitment to something *that is not guaranteed to work,* and in my experience, that scares a lot of church leaders. I get it. There is too much on the line financially, spiritually, and missionally to risk failure. Of course we don't want to take risks, even more so if we've had some "success." And so, instinctively, we choose to stick with the model of church that brought us "success" in the past. If in-person discipleship classes flourished in the past, we should go back to that well again, right? Or if a Vacation Bible School increased attendance a generation ago, we continue scheduling that every year. Or perhaps it was a quarterly worship night, potluck dinner after the evening service, Christmas pageant, creative conference, or family camp that once brought you some success, but now no one really knows why you continue to do it. So, we put a notice in the church bulletin announcing a six-week discipleship class, and wonder why only three people show up on the first week, two of whom have done the course half a dozen times already.

Right now, the Church needs to be more innovative than ever before, not because of COVID-19 in the world, but because of indifference in the world.

Grant goes on to write that taking risks is only appealing when we are facing a certain loss—like when a global pandemic forces church buildings to close and in-person services to be put on hold. In *Originals*, Grant shares the story of Harvard professor John Kotter, who studied more than 100 companies trying to implement major changes to their systems and strategies, only to fall short because there was no "sense of urgency" from company leaders. "The prospect of loss brings the go system online," Grant concludes. This proved true for the pastors who made the leap from analogue to digital in March 2020, in the face of loss of in-person services. But the irony is, we were facing loss of attendance long before March 2020, and we hadn't done a thing about it.

Right now, the Church needs to be more innovative than ever before, not because of COVID-19 in the world, but because of indifference in the world.

I agree with my friend, Carey Nieuwhof—best-selling author, leadership expert, and podcaster—who says, "If there's one thing the church needs today, it's more innovation in our methods. The mission never changes, but frankly, the methods have to." Now is *not* the time for us to go back to "how we've always done it," but to make an honest assessment of where we are now. We need to ask questions about why church attendance has been in freefall for years, and how we can connect with an already digitally connected generation.

Now is the time to be unwavering in your mission while experimenting with your model. It's time to ask questions about your church model, your church attendance, your church resources, and your church's ability to reach people in your local community. If you don't, you risk repeating a history of declining attendance. Now, unlike any other time in history, churches need innovative leadership in the digital space.

FEAR OF RESOURCES

Another fear I've heard expressed often from pastors is the Fear of Resources. Every time I speak at a conference or webinar about the need for churches to minister digitally to people, I usually get at least a dozen pastors who push back due to what they describe as a lack of time, money, and/or staffing to be able to pull off a digital or online ministry with excellence.

I totally understand this issue.

The majority of my hands-on ministry experience has been at mega-churches—churches with over 2000 attendees on Sundays—where, frankly, the resource issue just isn't as pressing. Smaller churches with a smaller church staff are usually juggling the multiple responsibilities that make up their overstuffed job descriptions, while mega-church staff are often allowed to specialize in a single specific area—like I was with social media. To the pastors expressing these concerns to me after a conference session or on social media or email, I usually share the same story.

In May 2020, just over a month after most church buildings in the U.S. were closed due to COVID lockdowns, I received a message from a church pastor from Texas. He told me how he'd been streaming his

Highly personal
>
Highly produced

Sunday services for about six months, and had been getting around 150 views each time from his church of roughly 400 people. Then, one afternoon as he took his dog for a walk around his neighborhood, he decided he wanted to pray for local residents. He pulled out his smartphone, opened the YouTube app, and started a livestream. As viewers started watching the stream, he asked them to leave a comment if they needed prayer, and as they did, he prayed for them by name, right there and then as he walked his dog.

By the time he finished the livestream about 30-minutes later, close to 12,000 people had tuned in to watch the impromptu prayer session!

He contacted me to ask why he had attracted so many viewers—many of whom were from the region in Texas where he lives and serves.

Good production will make quality content, but contextualized content will make a difference.

I told him there could be a number of different factors, but the most obvious one to me was this simple equation: Highly personal > highly produced. While his staff and volunteer media team worked all week to get about 50% of the church watching their Sunday live streamed service, he got 12,000 views while streaming from his phone as he walked his dog!

The lesson here is that you don't need a lot of fancy equipment or a big production crew to make an impact. Most of us are carrying around a $1000 camera in our pockets every day, but we still think we need a film crew to go live online. This pastor in Texas made a difference because he made it personal. His content was contextualized to the people watching.

Good production will make quality content, but contextualized content will make a difference.

FEAR OF COMPARISON

The resource issue was something Frank Blake talked with me about too, but for him it was less about the amount of resources, and more about the intent. "We were not the first company to take the Internet seriously, we were just one of the first to dedicate a lot of resources to it, including our best people," Frank told me. "I just saw that we needed to invest as much as we could toward this opportunity. Usually what you see is that the person in charge of an organization's online presence is not seen as someone who is central to the organization. And I think that's because we misidentify online as a generational challenge. We have to get the right people in place as a first priority. Then we have to make sure we get the other resource allocations right."

Which brings me to what I call the Fear of Comparison. In my experience, it seems a lot of pastors fear that if they stream their services online, they risk being compared to, and possibly shown up by, other pastors posting their own content online.

When COVID-19 first started impacting local churches, I had a number of pastors from the U.S. and the UK tell me they were concerned about taking their services completely online because they were worried that the people in their church community would start watching "celebrity preachers" online. They were concerned they would have to compete with world-class speakers from large, well-known churches. Or they would ask me how their church's volunteer worship team could compete if their church community started watching Hillsong Worship or Elevation Worship online.

When it comes to online and social media, context—not content—is king.

The truth was, many of the people in their churches had likely already been watching these teachers and worship teams online for years. COVID didn't start that phenomenon.

Still, I totally understand why church leaders would be concerned that they are now being compared to these highly influential, highly experienced, and highly gifted church leaders and communicators. But there is something a local community church pastor can do that these famous speakers could never do: serve the local community where they had been called.

Unlike these high-profile pastors that people often watch online, every local pastor has been called to serve the community where their church is located. And whether your local church is in Melbourne, Florida or Melbourne, Australia, you have been called to serve the people in your town or city!

My encouragement to every pastor reading these words is this: Instead of worrying about what some pastor in Atlanta, Georgia is doing, focus on equipping your church to meet the needs of the people in your local community in a way that only *you* can do. Then you won't ever have to worry about which "celebrity pastor" or which famous church the people in your community are watching.

A famous church in a different city might put out great content that can help the people in your city. But their content can only help so much, because that content is not contextual for your local community. And when it comes to online and social media, context—not content—is king.

These large churches with enormous budgets and a plethora of resources may be able to put out high quality, helpful content on a consistent basis, but they can't be relevant to the people who live within driving distance of your church—not relevant in the way I mean it. As much as we have come to associate the word "relevance" with moving lights and a smoke machine during a worship set led by a singer with skinny jeans and a deep V-neck shirt, it's about so

Being relevant is about meeting someone's need in the moment they need it.

much more than that. To put it simply, being relevant is about meeting someone's need in the moment they need it. But a bad definition of relevance will have us taking the bait that fear of comparison offers and keep us from doing what the world needs us to do.

Here's what I mean:

Imagine you are stranded in the desert for a week with no food, no water, and no way out. After seven days, you're tired, hungry, thirsty, and you know you don't have much time left. Then, in the distance, you see the dust cloud kicked up by an approaching car. At first you think it's a mirage, but you can soon hear the faint sound of the motor and you realize you're saved. As the car pulls up, and a person gets out with a bottle of water and some food, are you paying attention to what model the car is, or what the person is wearing? Are you wondering if the brand of water bottle is your favorite or if they have the sort of food you prefer? Of course not! None of that matters! This person is now the most relevant person in the world to you, because they have met your immediate needs.

CONTEXT IS KING

If you or your church can create content that meets the felt needs, or answer the questions, or provide the most needed resources to the people living in the community where your church is based and where you have been called to serve . . . then that content, by default, will be relevant. And with that, the fear of comparison loses its power. Even more than that, your content will engage and connect with the people in your specific CONTEXT.

A church that understands that context is king on social media, You-Tube, or podcasts will use these platforms to invite the people who live within a 30 minute drive of their building into life changing conversations instead of just inviting them to church events. Your content will only make a difference when you make CONTEXT the priority. And that's what will set you apart from the "celebrity" pastors and speakers you're worried everyone is watching online instead of you.

Which brings us to the next question: How do you learn about the felt needs of those living in your local community?

CHAPTER 05

THE ZERO MOMENT OF TRUTH

"

Science is about explanation. Religion is about meaning. Science analyzes, religion integrates. Science breaks things down to their component parts. Religion binds people together in relationships of trust. Science tells us what is. Religion tells us what ought to be. Science describes. Religion beckons, summons, calls. Science sees objects. Religion speaks to us as subjects. Science practices detachment. Religion is the art of attachment, self to self, soul to soul. Science sees the underlying order of the physical world. Religion hears the music beneath the noise.

RABBI JONATHAN SACKS

THE LAST TIME I PURCHASED a new camera, I had no intention of going to a mall, or visiting a brick-and-mortar store. So, my quest began with an online search. I got on my laptop, opened a new browser window, and typed the phrase: "what is the best camera to buy this year?" That was the beginning of my journey, which ultimately ended about two weeks later when a package arrived at my front door containing a new mirrorless camera body.

Whether it's buying tickets to a concert, streaming a movie at home, buying a new pair of shoes, or deciding which restaurant to go to for a night out, the Internet has forever changed the way people make decisions. Today, everyone is a digital explorer, which means that more often than not, we make decisions—regardless of how big or small—with the help of online ratings, reviews, and product descriptions.

We know it simply as online shopping, but to retail and marketing organizations, this sort of research *before* the shopping experience has become the foundation of their entire strategy.

Since 2011, multinational technology giant Google has referred to the process of researching online before making a purchase as the, "Zero Moment Of Truth," or "ZMOT" for short.

Google coined the phrase as a response to what former Proctor and Gamble CEO A. G. Lafley referred to in 2005 as "the first moment of truth"—when a consumer stands in a store deciding between two competing brands. The "second moment of truth," Lafley said, came when the consumer took their new product home, experienced it for the first time, and was either happy with their decision or not.

Six years later, Google announced that the Internet had created a new moment of truth that happened *before* a consumer even set foot inside a physical store. This new moment of truth, Google explained, came when a person first started researching brands and products online. A new Zero Moment of Truth was born.

According to Google's official book on the topic, *ZMOT: Winning The Zero Moment Of Truth*, a ZMOT is "a new decision-making moment that takes place a hundred million times a day on mobile phones, laptops, and wired devices of all kinds. It's a moment where marketing happens, where information happens, and where consumers make choices that affect the success and failure of nearly every brand in the world."

Since the introduction of this new concept, secular marketers and brands have been paying big money to ensure their products are at the top of the Google search engine results page (SERP, an acronym you'll want to know if you want to reach more people with the Gospel) when someone like me types "what is the best camera to buy this year" into my browser window.

ZERO MOMENT OF TRUTH IN RETAIL

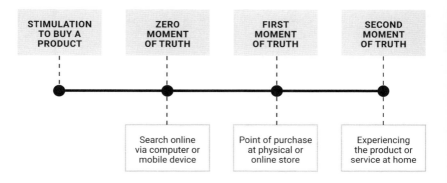

As pastors and church leaders, we also have a Zero Moment Of Truth when it comes to our "product." It happens anytime someone goes to their computer, gets online, and searches for things like:

How can I fix my marriage?

How can I be a better parent overcoming addiction?

How do I stop looking at porn?

How do I find hope?

ZERO MOMENT OF TRUTH IN CHURCH

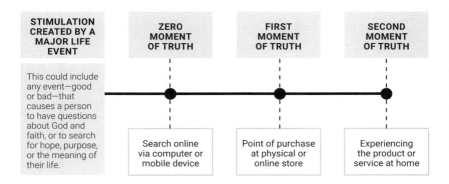

But people are no longer asking these questions about life and faith inside a church building. They are asking them online. And they are happening far more often than you think.

According to its own internal data[28], Google answers more than 100 billion searches every month. Software development company DOMO has drilled down a little further, revealing that between January 2021 and July 2021, 5.7 million Google searches were conducted every minute. This means that by the time you finish reading this paragraph, there will have been more than seven million searches on Google!

People aren't looking for local churches online or on social media anymore— they're searching for answers.

And no small number of those searches represent opportunities for church leaders to connect with real people who are asking real questions about faith in their moment of greatest need.

In addition to that, the ubiquity of smartphones and tablets means these moments are not just happening on a desktop or laptop computer, but increasingly on mobile devices. A national survey conducted in my homeland of Australia[29] by Mainstreet Insights shows that:

- 54% of Aussies are on their phones within three minutes of going to bed.
- 53% check their device within three minutes of waking up.

And, when this research focuses on millennials, the results show that 81% checked their phones within three minutes of waking up! While this research focused on Australians, I'm sure the numbers are similar in other parts of the world.

To me, all the insights listed above represent the biggest opportunity the Church has EVER had to engage with unchurched people who are searching for faith and hope.

People in your local community are more connected to technology than ever before, which means they're searching for answers via technology more than ever before. And because online searches are always accessible by anyone, from anywhere, at any time, people are having more zero moments of truth than ever before. But maybe most interesting of all is that according to research, the COVID lockdowns served to increase online searches around topics of faith.

Research from McCrindle[30] shows that in Australia, COVID led to one in three Aussies (33%) admitting they were more likely to engage with "spiritual conversations" in 2020, and two in five (41%) "thinking more about God." The team at McCrindle also found that 53% of Australians were thinking more about their own mortality in 2020, and 55% were asking questions[31] about "the meaning of life."

So, the question for you as a church leader is, when people in your local community go online in search of answers about the meaning of life, God, faith, and the Bible, or when they're looking for hope and purpose and meaning, are they connecting with your church?

You can actually check how your church is doing in the zero moment of truth *right now*. In fact, why don't you!? All you need to do is grab your smartphone or laptop, one of which is probably within reach (ami-right?!?) open up Chrome or Safari or Firefox or YouTube or *checks notes* Bing. Type in *"how do I read the Bible?"* or *"how do I become a Christian?"* and see if any content from your church comes up in the first page of the search results.

Probably not, right?!?

In fact, I'm so confident that your church's or pastor's content did not come up on the first page of the search results, that I'll give $100USD to anyone who can prove me wrong. And if your church or pastor's content comes up in the first three search results on the first page of results for either of these questions, I'll give you $50USD!

So let me ask you a question: Are you happy with what you see in the search results? Because whatever your search results show, this is what the people and families in your community are likely to see when they use the Internet to find the answers to their questions about faith and life.

Let me ask you another question: Short of typing in the actual name of your church, what would the people who live within driving distance of your physical building need to search for in order for your church to come up as the answer to their query?

People aren't looking for local churches online or on social media anymore—they're searching for answers. When people have questions about faith, they don't typically start by talking with a friend like I did when I first started having questions about God and the Bible, they start on Google or YouTube.

MY ZERO MOMENT OF TRUTH

I wasn't born into a Christian family, and I certainly didn't go to church when I was a kid. And while I occasionally had questions about God and the Bible growing up, all of my questions went unanswered because this was pre-Internet. That was until year 11 at high school, when I had to do a six-week project, ironically, in class called Computer Science, and I got paired up with one of our public school's three Christians. While I was initially annoyed at my bad luck at being paired with the kid who had Bible verses on his notebooks, and "JESUS SAVES" written in permanent marker on the bottom of his school bag, I ended up spending those six weeks peppering this kid with questions about God, church, Jesus, and the Bible. My project partner did his best to answer my questions, and when he didn't know, he told me he'd ask his dad who was a pastor.

That was my zero moment of truth.

By the end of those six weeks, that kid had answered my questions, invited me to a couple of church events, and given me the chance to experience Christian community. By the time our project was ready to be handed in, I had most of my burning questions answered, and had decided to start following Jesus.

That kid was there at my zero moment of truth when I had questions about faith and the Bible. He helped me find answers , and introduced me to an in-person Christian community. But in our 21st century world, followers of Jesus don't have to cross our fingers and hope we get paired up at school or work with someone who has a list of questions about faith. The digital revolution has given us a new place to reach unchurched people in whichever town, city, or community God has called us to serve in and people are hanging out there 24 hours a day, seven days a week, just waiting for you to help them in their zero moment of truth.

So the question is, what are you doing about it?

In the next section of this book I'll get super practical about *how* you can reach people searching for answers online. In chapter 8, I'll even specifically unpack how to find the faith questions people in your local community are asking, but before I do, let me highlight something important.

Most church leaders and pastors don't need *another* thing to do. Every day you are bombarded with messages telling you to do more online, create a YouTube channel, get a TikTok account, host a Zoom prayer meeting, start a podcast—the list goes on and on. I know firsthand how overwhelming this can be. Online ministry is my job and there are many times that even I feel like I'm getting buried in tech options. It's little wonder that in November 2021, Barna Research released a study showing that 38% of pastors have considered quitting[32] full-time ministry in the previous 12 months.

But I'm not writing this book to tell you what you're doing wrong.

My hope is that in this book you'll discover the opportunities you have as a church leader to make deep connections with people in your community and around the world. It's never been easier for us to reach people who are asking the sorts of questions we know Jesus can provide answers for. And because I want to make your job easier, in the next section I will provide detailed breakdowns of systems and strategies you can implement across multiple platforms. Hopefully, as you're intentional about using some of the tips in this book, you'll engage with people when they bring their deepest fears, their biggest concerns, and their most pressing needs to their search engines. In a world that's moving increasingly online, this is the easy, relevant, visible, and most effective way to reach the world.

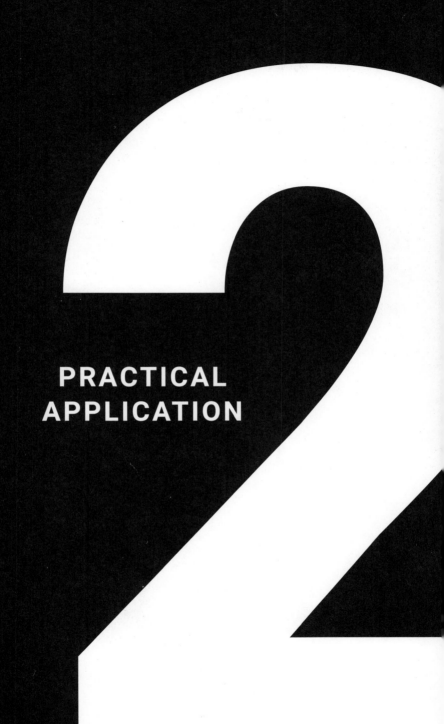

**PRACTICAL
APPLICATION**

CHAPTER 06

FROM MEGACHURCH TO METACHURCH

"

. . . church is not less than Sunday services, it is far more. It must be more to survive the Western spiritual apocalypse. Church must become a thick web of interdependent relationships between resilient disciples of Jesus deeply loyal to the Way.

JOHN MARK COMER, *LIVE NO LIES: RECOGNIZE AND RESIST THE THREE ENEMIES THAT SABOTAGE YOUR PEACE*

Megachurch[33]
noun
\\'me-gə-,chərch\\
: a church, usually Protestant, with a very large congregation (over 2000), typically housed in a complex offering sophisticated multimedia presentations and a range of secular facilities and services.

DEPENDING ON WHO YOU SPEAK to, the idea of megachurches either began in the 1970s when Robert H. Schuller opened the 2,890-seat Crystal Cathedral, in 1876 when famous evangelist D.L. Moody opened The Moody Church of Chicago (formerly Chicago Avenue Church) that could hold 10,000 people, or about 7 weeks after Jesus' death and resurrection when "about 3,000" were converted at Pentecost (Acts 2:41).

Regardless of when megachurches started, there is some evidence to suggest that the era of the megachurch is coming to a close.

In writing about megachurches in April 2021, author, church researcher, and founder and CEO of Church Answers, Thom Rainer, noted that, "The number of megachurches[34] has not grown over the past several years. They may have a larger share of the population of church attendees, but that movement may slow or even reverse in the next few years."

If Dr. Rainer is right and megachurches are moving toward extinction, what will take their place? Well, I believe future church leaders will not strive to build a megachurch, but a MetaChurch.

MetaChurch
noun
\\'me-tə-ˌchərch\\
: a group of Jesus followers who worship God and learn about their faith in a church building, small group, house Bible study, through video on-demand, podcast, or a live-streamed service and who still constitute one "congregation."

MetaChurch
verb
\\'me-tə-ˌchərch\\
: a body of Jesus followers who are actively developing and expressing their faith in their local communities, families, schools, sports and hobby groups, places of work, etc.—not just at a church building.

Okay, in full disclosure, this is a made up word I've been kicking around for a few years (for the record, long before Facebook changed its name to Meta). I'm not referring to a church located in Mark Zuckerberg's metaverse, or in AltspaceVR. And you won't find MetaChurch in Webster's. Yet.

The word "meta" is a prefix that can mean a number of different things. It can mean "to transform" as in *metamorphosis* or it can mean "to go beyond " or be "more comprehensive," as in *metaphysical* which means to go beyond the physical. When I use it as a prefix to the word "church" to create the word "Meta-Church," I am describing an expression of the Church that has been transformed to go beyond a church building or a Sunday time slot.

In other words, MetaChurch is an expression of "church" that gives meaning and validity to everyday faith experiences—whether they happen in-person, online, on Sunday, or throughout the week—and not just those that happen in a specifically designated building on certain days at a certain time. It refers to a group of Jesus followers who worship God and learn about their faith in:

MetaChurch is an expression of "church" that gives meaning and validity to everyday faith experiences—whether they happen in-person, online, on Sunday or throughout the week—and not just those that happen in a specifically designated building on certain days at a certain time.

- a church building,
- a small group,
- a house Bible study,
- video on-demand,
- podcast,
- or a live-streamed service,

who still constitute one "congregation."

A MetaChurch will also encourage people to worship God and actively express their faith in their local communities, families, schools, sports, and hobby groups, places of work, and not only at a church building.

This is key. A MetaChurch model is not just about using digital tools to connect people with content, but to engage with people online and offline to connect them with a community. At its core, the Church is community, not content.

While a MEGAchurch is one expression of Church with a large community, a METAchurch is multiple expressions of Church community (in-person, online, house church, virtual, etc.) with one mission.

Now, to be super clear, I am in no way against large churches or advocating for the end of megachurches! My wife and I worked in one of the largest, most influential churches in the U.S. and absolutely loved it! Megachurches have informed our ministry experience, strengthened our faith, and introduced us to lifelong friends. It's just that church leaders who focus more on getting people into a building than getting the Gospel to people by any means, will always see a pandemic as a threat to their mission. More importantly, they'll miss a growing opportunity to reach countless people who will never set foot in their building.

As mentioned in chapter 3, as of March 2021, 53% of U.S. adults do not attend a church, so we can't continue to expect people to automatically show up at our buildings—no matter what the seating capacity.

That's why I believe a MetaChurch model, of a fully integrated approach that seamlessly connects people to a 21st century church experience—whether they're online, using an app, or in a physical building—is the future of the Church. A MetaChurch approach to ministry fully engages people in a church community without necessarily requiring them to step inside a physical environment every single week. It takes the emphasis off connecting with people for just one hour on Sundays, and creates opportunities for church leaders to stay connected with people for the other 167 hours of the week online.

While a MEGAchurch is one expression of Church with a large community, a METAchurch is multiple expressions of Church community (in-person, online, house church, virtual, etc.) with one mission.

As my friend Kenny Jahng, Chief Innovation Officer for Big Click Syndicate, puts it, "Church should not be a pop-up shop that only shows up on Sundays. Digital has decoupled everything. You must think of church in terms of a series of interactions across the week, not a series of contiguous minutes within a specific hour on a Sunday."

Most importantly, a MetaChurch approach will also create opportunities for people to connect with faith and the church community in their zero moment of truth. MetaChurch creates

A MetaChurch approach to ministry fully engages people in a church community without necessarily requiring them to step inside a physical environment every single week.

an "omnichannel" version of church that can make the physical and the digital work together for the best possible outcome. Win-win! And as I mentioned in chapter 4, companies that do this are dominating the market and increasing their customer base—online *and* in-person.

In this sort of MetaChurch, leaders would have the opportunity to connect with people in their church community online *and* offline, while moving them toward full engagement.

This is an important and significant change—not just as Church models go but also in Church analytics. As Carey Nieuwhof says, "If you want your church to grow, stop trying to attract people, and start trying to engage people, because in the future, churches that engage people will have a far greater impact than churches that gather people." Engagement is the end in mind, and engagement can happen in more than one way.

FULLY ENGAGED

At North Point, we started adjusting our thinking around the idea of engagement in 2015. For the first 20 years of the church's history, North Point's vision was to "create churches that unchurched people love to attend." But as more people accessed our content online, the leadership team started to question the wording of that vision, because the measurement of success was based on people "attending." That's why, in 2016, the language of the vision changed to creating churches "where unchurched people love to engage."

While on the surface this may appear to be a social media unit of measurement, in reality, engagement at North Point is focused around four categories: participating in a small group, serving in a team, giving to the church financially, and inviting other people to church services and events. A person who is "fully engaged" at North Point is consistently participating in all four areas.

The first time I learned of these categories in a meeting, I started processing how many of these steps could be conducted or experienced online.

I knew we already had a large percentage of our church community supporting the church financially via apps and online giving after conducting a "Kick the Bucket" campaign a year earlier to remove offering plates from our Sunday services. As the online pastor, I also knew we had 70,000+ people watching our live streamed services every Sunday—many of whom shared the link to our services to invite their family and friends to watch with them.

My hesitation about online audiences being "fully engaged" in our church was around small group participation and serving in a volunteer team.

Our church online team had recently started gathering volunteers who interacted with guests watching our Sunday live stream. This was the start of an online volunteer team, but I was also aware this was often done in isolation, with people serving remotely from their homes. On paper it was an online volunteer team, but they didn't serve together in a physical online team environment.

Small group participation online was harder to quantify.

I knew anecdotally that many North Point small groups across Atlanta would occasionally video chat with participants who were out of town on business or vacation, but I would hardly call this an "online group." Earlier that year, my team and I had started experimenting with a strategy we called "City Groups," which involved connecting someone who watched our online services from a specific location with others who were watching from the same region.

This started when I first noticed that we had more than 120 individual IP addresses tuning in to watch our Sunday live stream each week from Anchorage, Alaska. So, we posted a stock photo of Anchorage to our North Point Facebook page, with a caption asking if there were any residents from the Alaskan city following the page. By the end of the week, we had more than 70 people identify as Anchorage locals, with many connecting directly with each other and making arrangements to meet together in-person.

> **Engagement is the end in mind, and engagement can happen in more than one way.**

A month later, after facilitating multiple connections, we noticed our IP count from Anchorage had dropped from around 120, to the low 70s—not because fewer people were watching, but because more people were watching *together* in a physical location from a single IP address.

We then started similar campaigns in South Carolina, Florida, Alabama, Louisiana, Texas, and the Virgin Islands. While these were not technically "online groups," they were physical groups made up of people who watched North Point's Sunday services online, and then, because of their proximity in a specific city or town, moved to off-line gatherings to discuss the messages.

The next step was to process if a similar approach to connecting people would be possible for the 100,000s of people who listened to our church podcasts every week. And if it was, could we develop a strategy of what a hybrid engagement pathway would look like for a person who engaged with our church both in-person and online?

That's when I developed the first iteration of what I now call the MetaChurch Engagement and Discipleship Pathway.

METACHURCH DISCIPLESHIP PATHWAY

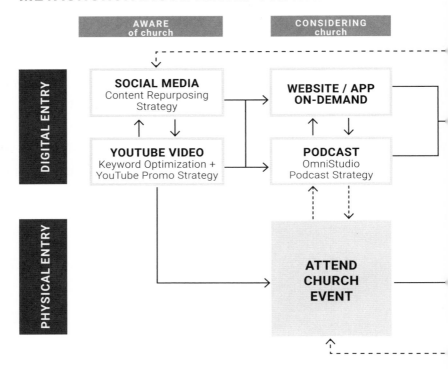

This MetaChurch Pathway outlines how a person moves from being aware of the church, to considering participation in the church community, to full engagement. It takes into consideration a person first connecting with a church in their zero moment of truth via a YouTube video or social media post, and outlines how they can move to being a small group participant, supporting the church financially, serving on a volunteer team, and inviting others into the church community.

I created the first version of this pathway in November 2017 at a time when more people than ever were accessing North Point's content digitally via live web streaming, video on-demand, podcasts, apps, and YouTube. These digital channels were not competing with physical attendance at our services; they were partnering with it.

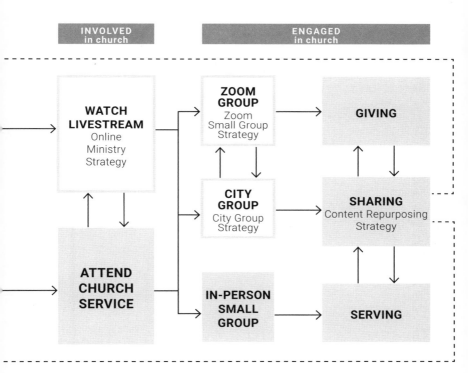

And since good leadership focuses on where we want to be, not where we were or where we currently are, the team at North Point understood that in order to continue making an impact in the postmodern world, we needed to adjust our model. We needed to create strong experiences that connected and engaged people on every channel they use to access our content—including physical attendance—so we could help inspire them to follow Jesus.

As church leaders, our past assumptions have to change to keep up with technology. In a world where people have an increasing number of online channels and apps to watch or listen to content, and ways to build community around that content, this model offers a new way to move seamlessly through physical and digital connection points on weekends and throughout the week. Likewise, a person—whose first connection with the church community is by attending an event or a Sunday service in-person—can easily stay connected to the community beyond these physical events via apps, video on-demand, live-streamed courses and classes, or podcasts.

Now, did this change in emphasis feel uncomfortable at the time? Did we wonder if we were making the right call? Yes. Of course! Change of any sort feels like a risk. But as Andy Stanley would tell the staff at North Point regularly, "Marry your mission. Date your model. Fall in love with your vision. Stay mildly infatuated with your approach."

Standing shoulder-to-shoulder with 100s of people in a church building at a specific time, singing songs, and watching a pastor speak uninter-rupted for 37 minutes is a *model*. But the *mission* of the Church is to preach the Gospel and make disciples. This mission can be achieved with various models.

Unfortunately, too many church leaders have gotten this backwards which, in part, explains why, for many pastors, utilizing technology in broader ways feels scary at best and wrong at worst. As Andy puts it, "Ministry models that no longer facilitate the mission of a church often become the mission of a church." So instead of looking for new models to reach more peo-ple and make disciples, many church leaders have inadvertently abandoned the mission in order to protect

> **The *mission* of the Church is to preach the Gospel and make disciples. This mission can be achieved with various models.**

their model at all costs. They've married the model and dated the mission. It's no wonder that, when COVID lockdowns started to ease and church buildings were open again, so many church leaders rushed back to their model of shoulder-to-shoulder physical services. They treated church online like a short term mission trip they were forced to do during COVID, but now they were back to the "real world."

When these pastors stepped back into their buildings, they also stepped back in time to the way things were—but with far fewer people sitting in front of them. A Pew Research study in March 2021[35] showed that 58% of U.S. church-goers had still not stepped back in the building since the COVID lockdowns.

And in June 2021, Gallup[36] research showed that church attendance in the U.S. was still at just 30%, the lowest it has ever been since records started in 1939.

My hope is, you're reading this book because you've realized what all leaders have to learn at some point or another: that scarcity breeds innovation. That the worldwide pandemic caused you to innovate—and that instead of pining about the past, you want to step forward into the future.

> **"I believe that the front door of the Church is now in a person's pocket. Most people's church experience actually starts in the digital world even if it finishes in the physical world."**

The good news is, I believe a MetaChurch approach is a step into that future. It understands how people access content and how they currently experience church, and it leverages every connection point to move them toward full engagement. Once connected with your MetaChurch community, all channels—both physical and digital—work together to move people toward experiencing services and encouraging them to connect in community and learn what it means to be fully engaged. That's because community is at the heart of the Church.

But it starts with how people first connect with your MetaChurch community.

Current president and CEO of Home Depot, Craig Menear, told Forbes in February 2020[37] that the retail giant had a new model for connecting with its customers (as previously discussed in chapter 4). They no longer expect people to simply walk into a store, but to start their interaction with Home Depot through a digital experience.

"We believe that the front door of our store is now in the customer's pocket," Menear said. "Most of our customer's experience actually starts in the digital world even if it finishes in the physical world."

This could be the quote of any lead pastor of a MetaChurch. It's certainly a quote I stand by, so I'll repeat: "I believe that the front door of the Church is now in a person's pocket. Most people's church experience actually starts in the digital world even if it finishes in the physical world."

Sure, some people may first connect with a church by walking in the front doors to attend an event or a Sunday service they've been invited to. But if the data already quoted from Pew, Gallup, McCrindle, and Barna is any indication, in the future, people will increasingly make their first connection with your church digitally.

The front door of your church is now in people's pockets.

This means people may connect to your church for the first time through a tweet or an Instagram Story. They may see a live stream on Facebook, or a TikTok video. Maybe their first connection with your church will be via a post on someone's Instagram grid featuring a quote from your Sunday message.

The front door of your church is now in people's pockets.

They may watch a 60-second YouTube Short, that leads to a 4-minute clip from your message on Twitter, which leads them to watch the whole 37-minute message on YouTube, which then leads them to watch an entire message series on your website—all before they set foot in your physical building.

In the postmodern world, new people connect *with* your church before they connect *within* your church.

But instead of staying anonymous online, this MetaChurch model ensures that people move into some variation of physical connection with the church community. This is what some Church thought-leaders have called "omnichannel church" or "hybrid church." I refer to it as "MetaChurch" because it is a transformed model that goes beyond the church building for an hour on Sundays, and into the community for the other 167 hours of the week.

MetaChurch does not just refer to *how* people connect with your church, but *when*. By leveraging technology, church leaders can engage daily with their community, not just on Sundays or during business hours. If the idea of creating constant, daily connection points with your church community still feels strange, check out one of the most quoted sections of the Bible when it comes to Church vision—Acts 2.

In the postmodern world, new people connect with your church before they connect within your church.

When I first got into full-time ministry, Acts 2:42-47 was quoted at me more times than I can count. Everyone in ministry loves the idea of a group of believers devoting themselves to teaching, gathering together in community, sharing everything and, most importantly, the final verse in the section where, "the Lord added to their number daily those who were being saved." We all love verse 47 because it is the ultimate pay-off to our "Sunday is coming" work ethic, right!? But Acts 2:46 says that in order to have God add "daily" to our church attendance, we need to meet together "every day."

"Every day they continued to meet together in the temple courts. They broke bread in their homes and ate together with glad and sincere hearts."
ACTS 2:46 NIV

Mark Batterson, New York Times best-selling author and lead pastor at National Community Church in Washington, D.C., highlighted this very idea in an interview with The Barna Group in September 2020[38]. "We all want Acts 2:47 when God added to his Church daily, but then we ignore Acts 2:46," Batterson said. "We want God to add to his Church daily while we gather weekly. It's not going to happen."

The good news is, in this day and age, meeting "every day" doesn't require your ministry staff to work longer hours. It just requires them to work smarter—and more creatively.

"Right now, God is giving us a gift. The gift is us asking, 'How do we be the Church every single day?'" Batterson said. "That's why [our church is] trying to innovate some ideas right now to make sure that we are a daily church, so that we live that out Monday through Friday."

Batterson and the team at National Community Church have surreptitiously become a model for a MetaChurch approach, creating multiple ways people in the local community can connect with the church on any day, on almost any channel. They meet in physical locations around the DC metro area, while also streaming Sunday services online. The church also puts out a daily podcast offering 5-minute devotions, hosts a daily prayer meeting at 7:14AM via Zoom called "The Upper Zoom," streams worship music to Spotify and Apple Music, and has an app that streams kids'

"Go into all the world and preach the gospel to every creature."

and student content. If that wasn't enough, small groups from National Community Church, which met online during 2020 or socially distant in parks, serve the local community by donating money for sleeping bags for the homeless, and wrote letters of encouragement to people in jails. And the church just recently opened the Phase Family Center, a 20,000-foot child development center to minister to local families by providing trustworthy and accessible child care.

"We've done a number of different things," Batterson says[39]. "Some of them are so simple. We do a bedtime story on Sunday nights on Instagram for NCC Kids. It sounds so simple, but those little personal touches during a season of social distancing are pretty meaningful."

This is a MetaChurch.

It's a model that is built on creating steps rather than programs. Every channel—whether online or in-person, on a website or in an app, physical or digital—works together to move people toward full engagement in the church community. A MetaChurch model not only requires all online channels and platforms to be working together with in-person physical attendance, but also that every step includes a call to action for the next step.

Hopefully by now you're starting to see the impact a MetaChurch model can have on people in your church community. We also know there are more people than ever not attending church at all. What do we do about them?

GO INTO ALL THE WORLD

This is where Mark 16:15 comes into the picture. Here, Jesus tells his followers—that's all of us—to: "Go into all the world and preach the gospel to every creature." That word "go" implies intentionality. It implies a strategy of deliberately going out into the world to find people and make disciples.

Now, it's important for you to know that after an exhaustive word study, I've learned that the biblical Greek and Hebrew words we translate as "go" throughout the Bible mean . . . "to go." Nothing more, nothing less. They mean GO! The Greek word for "GO" in this verse is "poreuo-mai" (πορευθέντες pronounced "por-yoo'-om-ahee" [Strong's 4198]), and the Hebrew word for "GO" is "halak" (הלך, pronounced "haw-lak" [Strong's 1980]). Both simply mean . . . "GO"!

Jesus was clear—we've got to GO. And in the postmodern era, going into "all the world" includes going on social media platforms like Instagram, Twitter, TikTok, and Facebook. It includes podcasts. It includes YouTube. To go into all the world in the 21st century is to deliberately post to these platforms with a purpose and intentionality to make disciples. Instead of seeing social media and online platforms as just a way to promote physical attendance, we can use them to promote spiritual disciplines. You don't make disciples by using social media to invite people to events and programs, but by using social media to invite them to life changing conversations and experiences, wherever they may be.

My friend Nona Jones, head of faith-based partnership at Facebook, put it this way in her book *From Social Media To Social Ministry: A Guide To Digital Discipleship*: "Jesus embodied 'GO' by never putting his name on any building, because he wanted to demonstrate through his life what ministry is all about: movement towards others."

Nona, who is a pastor of a church in Florida, put it this way in an interview with Carey Nieuwhof: "Somewhere in our history we started to think of church as a place and a program. We started to believe that 'church' was a location. But when Jesus was assembling his 12 disciples, he told them to 'come follow me, and I will send you out to fish for people.' To fish for people requires going out into the deep, but now, instead of going out to fish, the church has become an aquarium[40]."

In December 2021, I learned the difference between the open water and an aquarium. I got invited to scuba dive for the very first time, at a place called Osprey Reef in the Coral Sea, more than 300 kilometers off the coast of Australia. For my third dive ever, we did a drift dive along the wall of the reef, with a 2000 meter drop on one side, and the reef wall on the other. I saw more fish than I've ever seen in my life—not behind a glass panel, but swimming all around me! At one point, there was a school of giant trevally circling overhead, while what looked like a waterfall of bright blue and yellow fish poured over the reef wall and out of sight. Grey reef sharks, silvertips, loggerhead turtles, and giant cod fish swam by close enough to touch. The whole experience was exhilarating and frightening. It was life changing—and far beyond anything I'd experienced in an aquarium.

What kept me focussed and motivated in the midst of my open water fear was Pablo, the marine biologist and dive instructor just in front of me, and Jimmy, the National Geographic expedition leader swimming two feet away from me. Their guidance, leadership, and empowerment would not have been required in an aquarium, but in the open water surrounded by wild animals, they kept me calm, motivated, and safe.

In the same way, for a church to make the shift to a MetaChurch model requires a confident, self-assured leader who is not afraid to delegate authority. As Carey Nieuwhof says, "If you can be good with the fact that micro-gatherings, distributed gatherings, and people watching from home count, then you can mobilize those people in the same way you would people who are in your building."

I have no doubt that a MetaChurch model requires a rare breed of church leaders willing to rethink their approach to reaching people and taking on a complex model. But as I've heard Andy Stanley ask the staff at North Point and thousands of church leaders around the world many times, "What is the faith of the next generation worth?"

Because how we answer that question will determine how uncomfortable we are willing to get in trying something new in order to reach that generation. So, *what is the faith of the next generation worth to you?*

What is the faith of the kids in your preschool ministry, or the students in your youth ministry worth? What is the faith of your own children, your own grandchildren worth?

I think it is worth rethinking your current model—the model passed down to you years or maybe decades ago—so you can adopt a new model for doing church that reaches more people, and helps fulfill the mission of Jesus' church to "go into all the world and preach the Gospel to every living creature."

CHAPTER 07

FIRST CENTURY MISSION, 21ST CENTURY MODEL

"

Jesus said go and make disciples, but so often we just sit and make excuses.

AUTHOR AND PREACHER, FRANCIS CHAN

I ONCE ASKED A RABBI why he didn't believe Jesus was the Messiah.

The rabbi, a personal friend of mine from New Jersey named Rabbi Lubin, told me that while he believed Jesus was a great rabbi, he couldn't accept Jesus as Messiah because his followers have done so many destructive things in his name.

"Jews judge a rabbi based on the behavior of their followers," he said.

Read that again: *"Jews judge a rabbi based on the behavior of their followers."* This was the reason my friend didn't believe Jesus was the Messiah. He followed up by adding, "The behavior of the disciple reflects the authority of the rabbi."

If you're like me, that line felt a lot like a punch in the gut. As it should!

Now, with that thought ringing in your ears, what does it look like to "make disciples" who accurately reflect the teachings of Jesus? This is a question I've been processing almost every day since I started working in ministry. And finding the answer is critical because making disciples is our central calling as followers of Jesus. It's one of the key reasons the Church exists.

When I first started going to church as a 17-year-old, I thought being a disciple meant completing the six-week discipleship class my church held twice a year. And that's because the Hebrew word we translate as "disciple" in the Bible is "talmid" (דימלת pronounced "tal-meed"), which we usually translate as "student." But, as Rabbi Lubin taught me, while this word does mean "student," it can actually be translated as "apprentice"—someone who is being led to become just like their teacher. The translation of דימלת as student is correct, Rabbi Lubin told me, but the English concept of "student" doesn't quite cover the nuance of this important Hebrew word.

As most high school students know, if you can recite what the teacher says in class, you will get an 'A'. Think back to when you were a student in school and sitting in math class. The teacher was at the blackboard passing on information you knew you had to understand and memorize on some level in order to get a good grade or pass an exam. But this model doesn't make a student an apprentice. As any apprentice knows, it's not enough to be able to recite the lessons from the qualified tradesperson. They need to watch what the trades-person does, so they can follow their example in order to eventually be qualified themselves to do the work they learned. An apprentice mechanic, for example, not only watches the qualified mechanic at work, but also does what they see their teacher do, so that one day, they will be qualified to have their own garage!

Likewise, as apprentices of Jesus, we are to follow his example and reflect his teaching and understanding of Scripture in the world.

When Jesus started sharing his new perspective about God in first century Israel, he didn't just walk around publicly spouting his opinion and expecting people to change. He invited 12 young men to follow him, watch the way he lived 24-7, hear the way he spoke, and observe the way he served others. This is why he told them to "follow me," and it's what he meant when he said:

> *"The student is not above the teacher, but everyone*
> *who is fully trained will be like their teacher."*
> LUKE 6:40 NIV

This is what the Apostle Paul did with his friend Timothy. Paul walked alongside Timothy, discipling and mentoring him as they traveled together. This is what Paul meant when he said; *"Follow my example, as I follow the example of Christ." (1 Corinthians 11:1 NIV)*. It's also why Paul wrote to the church in Ephesus encouraging them to; *"Imitate God, therefore, in everything you do" (Ephesians 5:1 NLT)*.

A disciple of Jesus is someone who reflects Jesus.

This means, if you say you follow Jesus, everything you do today—every word and action, the way you drive, the way you respond to people at work, school, or the store, your attitude, and every social media post—should reflect Jesus. In my opinion, no one sums this up better than New York Times best-selling author Bob Goff, who says, "The best way to show people that God is everything we say He is, is for us to be everything He says we are."

Everything you do reflects the God you say you believe in. This is what it means to be a disciple.

And being an apprentice of Jesus means following his mission to *make* disciples. Jesus made this clear when he told us to *go* into all the world to preach the gospel (Mark 16:15) and make disciples (Matthew 28:18). So how does this work in a MetaChurch model? Well, I truly believe that for the first time in human history, we are able to fulfill Jesus' first century mission using a 21st century method.

Thanks to the Internet, social media, podcasts, apps, and YouTube, we can literally "go into all the world" in an instant and do exactly what Jesus said we should in Matthew 28:

> *"Therefore go and make disciples of all nations,*
> *baptizing them in the name of the Father*
> *and of the Son and of the Holy Spirit."*
> MATTHEW 28:19 NIV

MODERN-DAY DISCIPLESHIP

As discussed in the previous chapter, the Internet gives us the opportunity to stay engaged with people in our churches every day—allowing us the same opportunity Jesus had with his first century disciples. But two ideas can be simultaneously true:

1. Physical relationships are the catalyst for discipleship.
2. Physical relationships are enhanced through digital connections.

For example, we can stay connected with what people are doing via their social media feeds; they can see how we react to current issues in society through Twitter; they can see what makes us laugh on TikTok; we can provide them with daily teaching and encouragement through pre-recorded content or live streams on YouTube or podcasts; and the people in our churches have access to us and our personal lives via our own Facebook and Instagram accounts.

Quick side note on this last example: There's a difference between personal and private. The intimate relationship details of my family life or the confidential pastoral meetings I have with people at my church are private—these are not accessible to the public. I do not share these things on public-facing social media, and I would advise you to keep these things private also. However, being authentic and genuine on social media requires sharing "personal" things about myself, my struggles, and the things I'm learning.

The use of mobile devices and online technology gives us digital proximity to people.

Okay, back to the bigger idea, which is: Churches need to leverage social media, YouTube, and digital technology as *part of* a good discipleship strategy.

Crucial to that last sentence is the phrase: "part of." I didn't say, "Social media and digital technology is the backbone or foundation of any good discipleship strategy." I also didn't say, "You can completely disciple people online without the need to ever meet face-to-face in-person."

Based on what we know about how people interact with their digital world, moving forward, any good discipleship strategy will need to integrate a robust digital strategy to meet people where they live. Here's why.

People are increasingly using digital tools to build spiritual foundations.

The use of mobile devices and online technology gives us digital proximity to people. Jesus himself modelled that relationships are the catalyst for discipleship. In the context of the first century, this required Jesus to live 24/7 with his disciples for about three years, because physical proximity was the only way people could stay connected like that. *In the 21st century, technology allows us to enhance physical relationships through online connections*. When church leaders use technology as a tool for discipleship, we're able to turn digital spaces into sacred places for an individual (see chapter 5 for more).

Next, people are increasingly using digital tools to build spiritual foundations. Mobile devices and technology are such a natural extension of our daily lives, they've become an essential extension of our spiritual lives. And yes, there's data to support this.

In March 2020, Barna Research[41] released a report highlighting the impact of technology on faith formation, and found that 38% of Christians used social media to help grow their faith, which is the same as the number of people reading Christian books on faith-based topics. Barna also found that one in four practicing Christians listened to sermons on podcasts during the week, and the same number watched a sermon from their church on demand during the week. Among millennials, this number jumped up to one in three!

Our goal as church leaders is to turn people's smartphones from being a tool for distraction into a tool for discipleship.

Mark Batterson from National Community Church told me he believes church leaders need to catch up with what tech companies are already doing. "Our phones are discipleship devices, one way or the other," Batterson said. "You are already being discipled through technology because there are algorithms that are being designed to lead and direct us in a certain direction. So the question is, are we as church leaders leveraging technology, because everyone else is! We have to ask ourselves constantly how we can use the devices to foster discipleship."

David Kinnaman, president of Barna[42], says the trends his team uncovered in their 2020 study provided a window for church leaders into the future of faith practice. "Christian Millennials are more likely than older generations of Christians to report using digital tools to grow spiritually—such as listening to a sermon via podcast—even describing these kinds of things as a substitute for church attendance," Kinnaman said.

> **Digital discipleship is not about a completely impersonal, non-physical approach to spiritual formation—it's an integration of online and offline.**

"While that may read as a red flag to many ministry leaders, the data represent(s) those who agree strongly that faith is very important in their lives and have attended church at least once in the past month. So, even if nearly half of millennials substitute digital and other kinds of media resources for church attendance, they are still finding time to gather with a larger body of believers at least once a month."

This is the essence of a MetaChurch approach to discipleship—digital and physical working together, strategically.

You see, digital discipleship is not about a completely impersonal, non-physical approach to spiritual formation—it's an integration of online and offline. Digital discipleship is a life-on-life, follow-my-example-as-I-follow-Christ apprenticeship, with digital elements and content included to enhance connectivity.

According to Kinnaman, this gives those of us in ministry a choice: "Church leaders can respond by providing thoughtful integration of digital tools, strategies, and content into their spiritual development efforts. Ultimately, millions of practicing Christians—and especially younger Christians—are telling us they are comfortable with these transitions, whether church leaders are or not."

If we assume that because we prefer to meet and connect with people in-person, that this is what everyone prefers or what's best, we risk missing opportunities to connect with people who are

Your neighbor is not just the people who are like you, but also the people who are *nothing* like you!

wired differently. Using online tools may not personally be *our* first choice when it comes to discipleship, but it is often the best choice based on who we're hoping to serve.

Remember, your neighbor is not just the people who are like you, but also the people who are *nothing* like you!

Finally—and this one might catch you by surprise—people are more authentic online.

Before you roll your eyes and throw this book across the room in frustration, let me explain.

As a pastor, I've been part of many counseling conversations with people to discuss everything from relationship issues and personal addictions, to theological questions and career advice. In almost all of these sessions, anywhere from 30-70% of the allotted time is consumed with small talk as people work up the courage to explain why they're *really* meeting with the pastor.

This became such a common occurrence that if a young single man wanted to "have coffee" with me, before they'd taken their first sip of their grande, three pump, skim milk, lite water, 2% foam, extra hot chai tea latte, I had already asked: "So, what is the thing you hope I *don't* ask you about today?"

But, when people contacted me via online service chat, email, or social media DM, they typically got straight to the point. Instead of beating around the bush, the separation provided by a digital interaction meant they felt more comfortable more quickly. And this is supported by research.

According to a study done by Stanford University[43], people are actually more honest online.

According to Jeff Hancock, the founding director of the Stanford University Social Media Lab and a professor in the Department of Communication, research into deception in the digital age, the different ways we lie, and how technology is impacting trust in communities,

People are more authentic online.

shows that people are more likely to lie offline than online. He says his team at Stanford has found that "communication tends to be more honest online, and this is in part because those messages are recorded and come from people that we will have future interactions with. We don't want a reputation as a liar, and it's easier in some ways to get caught in a lie online."

These Stanford findings are supported by Barna research[44] in September 2020 that found 87% of Christians who had participated in online discipleship programs such as webinars, courses, and small groups, said the digital environment provided "a safe space to speak openly."

We've already agreed that discipleship is about transformation. Having the ability to draw more honest information from the people we're discipling allows us to be more efficient and direct with our communication.

Discipleship has been the mission of the Church since the first century, and technology, social media, YouTube, and other digital tools give us a 21st century model to carry out that mission. When these tools are integrated with physical, offline relationships, they can help your church's discipleship strategy in three key areas:

- They give us increased access to people.
- They integrate seamlessly into people's everyday life.
- They make communication more honest and efficient.

A digital discipleship strategy is NOT a solely online experience. It's also a lot more than:

- having a social media content calendar
- streaming your church services online

- starting a Facebook Group for your church
- having a digital marketing budget
- posting sermon quotes to Instagram

Yes, some of these things can be part of a digital discipleship strategy, but when we limit the definition of digital discipleship to this list, we miss the point of discipleship. Likewise, when the *discipleship* capacity of a church is limited by the *seating* capacity of a church building, we've missed the point of Jesus' command to *go make disciples*. Discipleship is apprenticing people to be like Jesus, and as former Life.Church online pastor[45], Alan George says: "Discipleship is not a location-specific event or experience. It is every day, all day, and lasts a lifetime."

THINKING BEYOND SUNDAY

So now that we agree what discipleship is, and what a digital discipleship plan is not, how do we integrate online technology and social media into our church discipleship plan? Well, it starts with thinking beyond Sunday. If we want God to add more people "daily" to our church community (Acts 2:47), then we have to be prepared to meet together "every day" (Acts 2:46). This means developing points of connection between your church pastoral staff and your church community every day that go beyond the content you're posting on social media. It may mean starting a new 10-minute weekly Bible devotion podcast, or developing church-wide Bible reading plans. It may include Zoom prayer meetings, developing and recording an online Bible survey class, or doing a Bible study via YouTube livestream or the Instagram grid. It should include written content like blog posts and email campaigns, as well as parent resources and content for kids and students.

> When the *discipleship* capacity of a church is limited by the *seating* capacity of a church building, we've missed the point of Jesus' command to *go make disciples.*

Visually, this strategy may look like the following chart.

MIDWEEK CONTENT SUGGESTIONS FOR A METACHURCH DISCIPLESHIP STRATEGY

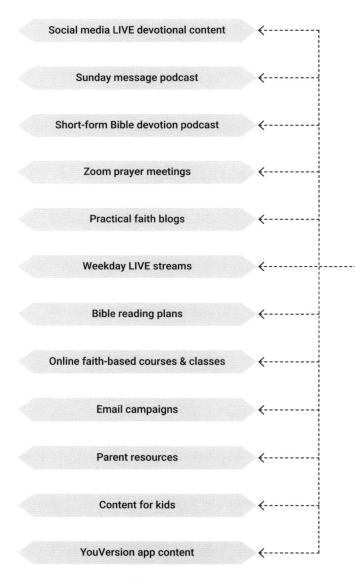

Social media LIVE devotional content

Sunday message podcast

Short-form Bible devotion podcast

Zoom prayer meetings

Practical faith blogs

Weekday LIVE streams

Bible reading plans

Online faith-based courses & classes

Email campaigns

Parent resources

Content for kids

YouVersion app content

MIDWEEK CONTENT

METACHURCH DISCIPLESHIP STRATEGY

The front door to your church is in people's pocket

Some of this could be online-only, some onsite-only, and some may be a hybrid of both. The point is to create daily opportunities for people to engage with your church.

Now, to be super clear, I'm not suggesting that every church do all of this every week! And I'm not suggesting that this is a comprehensive list of all the content opportunities a church has. What I'm trying to do is provide a few suggestions for content that could form part of a digital discipleship strategy. The main point is that this content would sit outside of the Sunday onsite service experience.

If Dallas Willard is right—and I think he is—that, "discipleship is the process of becoming who Jesus would be if he were you," then we need to understand that the "you's" of today are more likely to integrate technology into their personal faith journeys. And this means, as church leaders hoping to disciple these new "you's," we need to integrate technology into our discipleship strategy.

Nona Jones from Meta puts it this way: "Discipleship requires us to reimagine our role in ministry so that we don't stop at waiting for people to find us before connecting with them. Discipleship compels us to go find them."

Going to find people so we can preach the gospel to them, and then disciple them, requires us to go to where they are. This is why social media, podcasts, online streaming, and digital access to groups form a key part of MetaChurch Engagement And Discipleship Pathway I outlined in the previous chapter. If church leaders are going to take seriously the call to "go" to make disciples, then we need to accept that going into the postmodern world includes going to places like Instagram, TikTok, Twitter, Facebook, and Twitch because this is where people already are.

And more than any other digital place, people are on YouTube all day, everyday. Next, let's explore how to leverage YouTube for your discipleship strategy.

CHAPTER 08

YOUTUBE YOUR CHURCH

"

The Church must be forever building, for it is forever decaying within and attacked from without.

T.S. ELIOT

IF THERE'S ONE THING I have learned from well over a decade as an online and social media pastor, it's that YouTube is the most important platform for any church leader wanting to use digital tools to make disciples.

This became obvious to me the last time my car broke down.

A few years ago, on a sweltering summer day in Atlanta, I went to my garage to start my normal commute to work. But when I turned the ignition key in my 2008 Chevy Impala, a high pitched clicking noise came screaming from under the hood, and the car didn't start. I tried again, and was greeted by the same high pitched noise. I tried a third time, and the engine finally turned over and the car sputtered to life.

Realizing something was obviously wrong, and not wanting to drive my car 20 minutes south to work if there was a chance it would break down, I sat in my car and opened the YouTube app on my phone, searching for "high pitched clicking noise when starting the car." Genius, right!?

The video at the top of the search engine results page (SERP) was titled: "Car Won't Start & You Hear a Clicking Noise." It was 4:03 long. The second video was titled: "Car Clicks When Trying to Start? 5 Common Causes" which was 1:39 long. The third YouTube video was called: "Why Is My Car Making a Clicking Noise When Starting?" and was 1:04 long.

Naturally I clicked on the third and shortest video (why would I waste an additional 35 seconds of my morning??) and learned that my car battery was dying. I backed out of my garage and drove to the church office, stopping on the way at a car battery store (I doubt that's the official name). I kept the car running as I went in, bought a new battery, and then continued on my way to work. At lunch time, I went out to the parking lot to see if my car would start, and this time the clicking persisted and the engine would not turn over. So I popped the hood, replaced the battery, and the car was back in action for my commute home later that day.

Thanks to YouTube, my issue was solved.

What does this have to do with the Church? Stick with me.

In today's world, YouTube is the place people go to find the answers to everything: from fixing their car, to fixing their marriage. When life gets complicated, there is a generation of people who turn to YouTube—not the Church—for solutions.

Just a quick look at some of the statistics around YouTube at the time of writing reveal why this is the case:

- YouTube has 2.3 billion monthly active users.[46]
- 95% of people aged 18-29 say they regularly use YouTube.
- 91% of people aged 30-49 say they regularly use YouTube.
- 83% of people aged 50-64 say they regularly use YouTube.[47]
- 50% of Gen Z say they can't live without YouTube.[48]
- 67% of Millennials believe they can learn anything they need to know about life from YouTube.[49]
- 37% of all mobile Internet traffic is people using YouTube.[50]

If this wasn't enough, YouTube is also the second biggest search engine in the world, owned by the biggest search engine, Google. In addition, in April 2021, Pew Research revealed that YouTube was the most widely used social media platform in the world, with 81% of adults actively using it, compared to 69% for Facebook[51].

> **In today's world, YouTube is the place people go to find the answers to everything: from fixing their car, to fixing their marriage.**

I have three daughters born just after 2000, so they have grown up with YouTube. This means they've grown up making major life discoveries and major life decisions on YouTube. If and when they turn to YouTube to search for questions about life, faith, hope, and following Jesus, I want to make sure they find helpful information from church leaders like you!

YouTube represents one of the greatest technological opportunities the Church has ever had to advance Jesus' mission of going into all the world to preach the Gospel and make disciples since the invention of the printing press.

Yes, you read that correctly. YouTube represents the greatest technological opportunity for the Church since German goldsmith Johannes Gutenberg invented the printing press around 1440.

But in order for us to take advantage of this technology, church leaders need to learn how to leverage YouTube—in the same way we've leveraged the printing press to create a Christian book industry[52] worth more than $640,000,000 a year in the U.S.

The first step in this process is to approach YouTube with intentionality and strategic thinking—not just as a place to upload a video of your Sunday message—though that's a great place to start.

YouTube is, first and foremost, a search engine, second only to their parent company, Google. If you want your content to be at the top of the search engine results page when someone goes online to ask the tough questions of life, then you need to leverage YouTube for what it is.

Instead of simply uploading a video and hoping for the best, you can optimize your content like you would for any search engine. By taking a few simple steps to strategically optimize your videos, YouTube will actually start to recommend your message videos whenever a person is searching online for the answers to the tough questions of life they're already asking in their zero moment of truth. (See chapter 5 for more.) This happens when we optimize our videos with keyword titles.

And the good news is, this is easier and cheaper than you think.

It doesn't require a huge media or production team, it works no matter where you are located, the size of your church or your staff team isn't important, and it doesn't require vast financial resources. In fact, the only thing it will cost you is a willingness to put away old thinking. And it starts with this idea: keyword titles.

KEYWORD AND KEYPHRASE TITLES

Over the past 30 years, I've been a part of three churches, and at each of these churches, I've been a part of the creative team that decided the titles for individual messages and message series. Back when I started, the way we titled messages was fine. Alliterations, clichés, and single word titles were the norm, and this worked well enough when all people did was show up to a building to access our content. But the Internet—specifically Google and YouTube—changed all of that.

Today, if you hope to reach the people at their zero moment of truth, you need to be leveraging keywords and keyphrases when deciding message and series titles.

So, what's a keyword? A keyword is a word that a person types into a search engine that the algorithm uses to match search results. For example, if a person types in the word "covid," a search engine will provide the top ranked searches that match that word, cross-referenced with the person's location and previous search history. As search engines became more sophisticated, two or more keywords could be used to generate a search. For example, "covid symptoms" would produce a different search engine results page than the word "covid" on its own.

Similarly, a *keyphrase* is a set of words that form a phrase people type into the search bar. This is the next step up from a keyword, and makes a search more specific. For example, a keyword search for "chicken soup" would produce a certain type of search; whereas, "easy chicken soup recipes" would be a keyphrase search that produced a more specific search result. Increasing the "tail" of that keyphrase to "easy chicken soup recipes in under 20 minutes" would change the result again. The more specific the keyphrase, the more specific the search results.

At North Point in 2018, I got the greenlight to run an experiment on message titles on our YouTube channel. The experiment involved renaming messages that Andy Stanley had preached that were at least six months old. I started with a single message that Andy had titled "Fish Tricks," which focussed on the story in the Gospels of Jesus calling fishermen to follow him and how nothing in our past disqualifies us from becoming a follower of Jesus.

I'll assume you know where this is going. No one will ever type "fish tricks" into the search bar on Google—unless they want to find a weird video of someone trying to teach their fish to play basketball[53] of course. I knew I had to change the title to something that lined up with what the message was actually about.

So, after doing a keyword and keyphrase search, I retitled the message to this: "Who Can Follow Jesus?" The result was almost instant. After two weeks, the newly titled video enjoyed a 45% increase in views, and a 60% increase in viewer retention. The increase in new views came from YouTube recommending the video when people typed either "follow Jesus" or "who can follow Jesus" into the search bar. The increased retention was the result of the video answering the question people were actually searching for.

Armed with the success of this single message, I expanded the experiment to an entire message series. The series I chose was called "You're Not The Boss Of Me: Putting Unhealthy Emotions In Their Place," and was six weeks long.

When I did a search, the phrase "you're not the boss of me" averaged about 210 searches per week. So, leveraging free, built-in Google tools like trends.google.com and ads.google.com, and paid services like monringfa.me, I found that the phrase "managing your emotions" pulled more than 700 searches per week. Next I tried the phrase "controlling your emotions," which at the time was attracting about 3000 searches a week, more than 10 times the original title! Finally, I did a search for the phrase "how to control your emotions," which had well over 8000 searches every week. So, I changed the title of the message series to "How To Control Your Emotions," and used keyword and keyphrase searches to rename all six messages in the series.

After just 30 days, this series had a 98% increase in viewing time on the church's YouTube channel. Again, people watched these newly titled messages for longer because the content matched what they were actually searching for online.

Sure, these titles may not have been as "catchy" or even as memorable as the old titles, but they were getting more views than ever before. And at the end of the day, the creativity of our titles doesn't matter if people can't ever find our messages online to watch them!

This was the start of a process I called "YouTubing your church"— getting the most from YouTube content by creating more searchable titles for messages, before they go online.

The next step after optimizing message titles is to optimize the videos themselves, and then the channel.

UPLOADING VIDEOS TO YOUTUBE

If you want to get the most out of YouTube, you need to start with a checklist of items that will help get you more views, longer view times, better click-through rates on your thumbnails, and even drive traffic to your social media channels.

This makes YouTube a key first step in the MetaChurch strategy.

The first item on this checklist is writing a default YouTube description for all new video uploads (a process undertaken through YouTube Studio). This default video description needs to include relevant calls to action and live links to your church social media channels and website. Here's an example of what a default video description for a church message could look like:

> In this video, ***<NAME>*** discusses ***<TOPIC>***, and how if you ***<ANSWER>*** it will help you ***<OUTCOME>***.
>
> Like, comment, and subscribe to stay updated with the latest content from ***<PASTOR'S NAME>***!
>
> CONNECT WITH ***<CHURCH NAME>*** HERE AT:
> - Instagram: https://www.instagram.com/***churchhandlehere***
> - Facebook: https://www.facebook.com/***churchhandlehere***
> - Twitter: https://twitter.com/***lotecommunity***
> - Website: https://***churchwebsitehere***
>
> #churchnamehashtag #churchlocationhashtag #serieshashtag

You can set this up in YouTube so it automatically preloads for every video you upload to your channel.

This is the start of a list of standard operating procedures (SOPs) for every video you've uploaded to YouTube, designed to give each new video the best possible chance to attract views.

Over the years, I've updated, tweaked, and dialed in an SOP list and shared it with 100s of churches around the world through Orange, a church strategy company based in Atlanta, and ministries in North America and Australia, including Carey Nieuwhof, YouVersion Bible app, Compassion International, and Alpha Australia.

YOUTUBE VIDEO UPLOAD CHECKLIST:

1. **Change video file name to optimized title before uploading.**
   The YouTube algorithm analyzes the filename of your video, so adding keywords to the file name optimizes the metadata of your video, helping it get to the first page of search results. And the words in the file name should be separated by hyphens to make them more SEO friendly. For example, a message video called "How To Get More From The Bible," should be uploaded with the file name, "how-to-get-more-from-the-bible."

2. **Give your video a keyword or keyphrase title.**
   As already discussed, keyword titles will improve views and viewer retention.

3. **Add a keyword description.**
   YouTube relies on video descriptions to help determine the content of your video, which is why it's important to add content-specific keyphrases to the description. While YouTube allows 5000 characters in the description, only the first 160 appear as a preview, so the first sentence or two should be the most optimized.

4. **Add a custom thumbnail.**
   According to YouTube, 90% of top-performing videos[54] use a custom thumbnail instead of the automatic screen grab YouTube generates upon upload. And studies have shown[55] people are up to 72% more likely[56] to click on a thumbnail if it includes a picture of a person's face.

5. **Add video specific tags.**
   Another way YouTube determines the content of your video is through video tags. Research shows[57] adding video-specific, keyword-rich tags to your videos will improve their ranking and help with search and discovery.

6. **Add a YouTube end screen.**
   YouTube ranks your channel based on view time—specifically, how long people spend on the platform after watching your content. This is why using end screen elements to encourage people to watch more content will help improve the ranking of your content.

End screens also allow you to prompt people to subscribe to your channel. Here's what an end screen looks like:

7. Add YouTube Cards.

YouTube allows you to add cards throughout a video to point people to additional content, similar videos, or an external website. They appear in the top right hand corner of a video and can be added at any point throughout your content. Here's how they look on a video:

YouTube cards are a great way to add a call to action on your video, and can be added in multiple places.

8. Add the video to a Playlist.
Before making the video live, make sure you add it to a YouTube Playlist to make it easier to find. Playlists live on the homepage of your YouTube channel and allow your videos to be grouped together. This means they are easier to find, but also allows your audience to access multiple videos around the same topic.

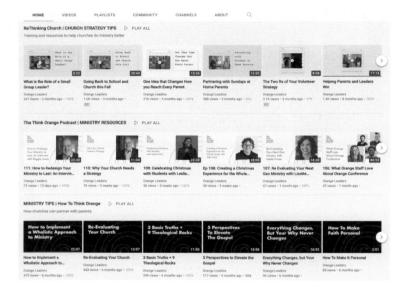

9. Review the video once live.
Once your video is live on your channel, there are several steps you should take as part of a video review in order to give it the best chance to be discovered. This review includes:

- **Watch the entire video.** This gives the video a 100% viewer retention rate right from the outset.
- **Give the video a "thumbs-up."** This generates engagement ranking on the video.
- **Add a comment.** This comment should be in the form of a question that encourages viewers to engage with the video.
- **Pin your comment.** Pinning your comment to the top of the feed means everyone who watches the video will have the chance to respond to your question.

10. Promote the video on social media channels.
Having a detailed YouTube video promotion strategy will help attract views, and extend the shelf-life of your content. This strategy should include multiple posts across multiple platforms, and should stretch beyond the week that video is posted to YouTube.

On the next page is a video promotion strategy I've developed and shared with churches and ministries around the world.

11. Ongoing engagement and testing.
Once a video is uploaded, there are several aspects that can be edited to continue to improve the ranking of the video. These include switching out thumbnails, re-editing the video title, and re-editing the video description. I recommend tracking a handful of key analytics to regularly test the video's searchability, making adjustments as required. And trust me, it's not as complicated as it sounds. We'll unpack that next.

KEY YOUTUBE ANALYTICS

YouTube Studio provides a variety of in-depth data analytics that can be used to monitor the success of a video, and improve its ranking and searchability. The data offered can be overwhelming, so I advise churches to focus on six key metrics to track for every video you upload. These are:

1. **Click-through rate (CTR):** This tracks how often viewers watched a video after seeing a thumbnail or video title. A normal click-through rate is 2-5%, 5-10% would be considered high, and anything over 10% is outstanding. Tracking CTR is important because YouTube allows you to switch out the thumbnail and change the title of a video as many times as you want. A video that is performing below average can become highly viewed content by changing one or both of these elements.

Before I move on, let's unpack thumbnails a little more. (In any other generation, that sentence would sound really strange). In 2016, Netflix released a report[58] on the power of thumbnails which revealed that various internal studies showed that the company had 90-seconds to grab a person's attention, otherwise, "that member will likely lose

YOUTUBE PROMOTION STRATEGY

New Video Posted

TWITTER

| Twitter promo 1 | Twitter promo 2 | Twitter promo 3 |

FIRST DAY

Twitter 341 Strategy
Promote YouTube link on Twitter three times on the first day the video is live, using unique copy for each tweet. Each tweet should promote a different aspect of the video content.

| Twitter promo 4 | Twitter promo 5 |

FIRST WEEK

Twitter 247 Strategy
Promote YouTube link on Twitter twice a day for the first week the video is live. These tweets should vary from each other, and be tracked to test which wording gets the most reach and engagement

| Twitter promo 6 | Twitter promo 7 |

FIRST SIX MONTHS

Twitter 246 Strategy
Promote YouTube link on Twitter twice a month for the first six months the video is live. These tweets will be based on the best performing tweets from the first week promotion

INSTAGRAM

Story with Link Sticker

Use a 9x16 variation of the YouTube thumbnail as the graphic. Use the Instagram Link Sticker to connect to video.

Short-form video edit to Reels

Short-form video edit to Grid

A 60-second highlight or bottom line edited from the full-length video, with "link in bio" CTA.

Grid Graphic

4x5 variation of the YouTube thumbnail, with "link in bio" CTA.

2nd Short-form video edit to Grid

A new 60-second highlight from the full-length video.

Grid Graphic

4x5 screen grab from video or custom graphic.

Story with Link Sticker

Instagram 246 Strategy
Post two Instagram Stories every month for the first six months the video is live. Use Link Sticker to drive traffic to the new video content.

LINKEDIN

Short-form video edit to LinkedIn

A 60-second highlight or bottom line edited from the full-length video posted to Linke-dIn feed along with YouTube link.

BLOGS

Blog post from video with video embedded

FACEBOOK

Page promo post

FB story posts

Group promo posts

Facebook will reduce the reach of posts that include YouTube links. For this rea-son, Facebook posts should include the YouTube thumb-nail or short-form video and caption, with the YouTube link placed in the second comment on the post.

Feed graphic

4x5 variation of the YouTube thumbnail, with YouTube link included.

Content Requirements for YouTube Promotion Strategy

1. 5–7 **Tweet** variations for testing, with and without graphics
2. Two 4x5 variations of YouTube thumbnail for **Instagram**, **Facebook**, and **LinkedIn**
3. Two 9x16 variations of YouTube thumbnail graphic for **Instagram** and **Facebook Stories**
4. Two 4x5, 60-second highlight edits of video content for **Instagram**, **Facebook**, and **LinkedIn**
5. Blog post copy, which could be a transcription from the original video

Feed graphics

LinkedIn 246 Strategy
Post a 4x5 screen grab from video or custom graphic twice a month for the first six months the video is live, along with the YouTube link.

interest and move onto another activity." Since the human brain can process images in as little as 13 milliseconds[59], Netflix doubled down on creating and testing thumbnails for movies and programs, because artwork was the biggest influencer in a person's decision to click on content. "We also saw that users spent an average of 1.8 seconds considering each title they were presented with while on Netflix," the report stated. "We were surprised by how much impact an image had on a member finding great content, and how little time we had to capture their interest."

This lines up with the words of the great presbyterian revivalist Charles Finney (1792 - 1875), who once said that every preacher should have "the Bible in one hand, and the map of the human mind in the other," because we need to understand the Bible *and* understand how to reach people. I bet Finney would crush his YouTube thumbnails!

Okay, now back to the analytics.

2. **View duration:** View duration is the total watch time of your video, divided by the total number of video plays, including replays. This metric measures your video's ability to engage viewers. After helping churches and ministries of all sizes from around the world with their YouTube channels, I've learned that the average retention rate varies, but if your viewer retention is above 45%—this means just under half the people who started watching the video were still watching at the end—then you're crushing it! To drill down a layer deeper, if your video is less than five minutes, and your audience retention is at or above 50%, you're doing an amazing job. If your video is longer than 5 minutes, and your audience retention is above 55% after the first 30 seconds, then your video can be considered successful.

3. **Watch time:** The amount of time viewers have spent watching your videos is considered the watch time. The difference between view duration and watch time is that view duration tracks the **_average_** amount of time people spend watching your videos, while watch time tracks the **_total_** amount of time viewers spend watching your videos.

Watch time is a channel-wide statistic, and every church should establish a baseline for a month, and then try to increase that watch time over the following months. I also recommend measuring certain months or seasons against the same period in previous years. For example, Easter season watch time should be measured against Easter the previous year.

4. **Views:** The views analytic tracks the number of legitimate, audience initiated views for your videos. More views indicates the overall success of a video's content. Views can be influenced by several factors including how you're promoting the video on other channels such as social media, the thumbnail, or the keyword title. Again, I recommend establishing a baseline over a month.

> **A fully optimized video on YouTube addresses the questions your audience is asking online, provides engagement opportunities, and is easily discoverable in a search.**

5. **Subscribers:** A YouTube subscriber is someone who has chosen to "follow" your channel and your content so they can stay updated with your latest videos. Subscribing to your channel should be a key call to action on every church's YouTube channel. Other calls to action include liking the video using the thumbs up icon, leaving a comment on the video, and sharing the video link on social media.

6. **Velocity:** Velocity tracks how quickly a specific video is getting organic views. The faster a video gets views from the moment it is published, the more that video is promoted to new viewers. YouTube provides a baseline for the channel after various time frames across a month.

On the following page is a general overview of these analytics and how to find them in the YouTube Studio.

KEY METRICS TO TRACK ON YOUTUBE

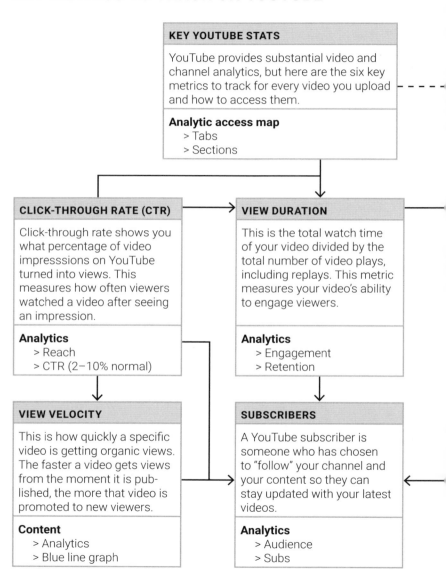

KEY YOUTUBE STATS

YouTube provides substantial video and channel analytics, but here are the six key metrics to track for every video you upload and how to access them.

Analytic access map
> Tabs
> Sections

CLICK-THROUGH RATE (CTR)

Click-through rate shows you what percentage of video impresssions on YouTube turned into views. This measures how often viewers watched a video after seeing an impression.

Analytics
> Reach
> CTR (2–10% normal)

VIEW DURATION

This is the total watch time of your video divided by the total number of video plays, including replays. This metric measures your video's ability to engage viewers.

Analytics
> Engagement
> Retention

VIEW VELOCITY

This is how quickly a specific video is getting organic views. The faster a video gets views from the moment it is published, the more that video is promoted to new viewers.

Content
> Analytics
> Blue line graph

SUBSCRIBERS

A YouTube subscriber is someone who has chosen to "follow" your channel and your content so they can stay updated with your latest videos.

Analytics
> Audience
> Subs

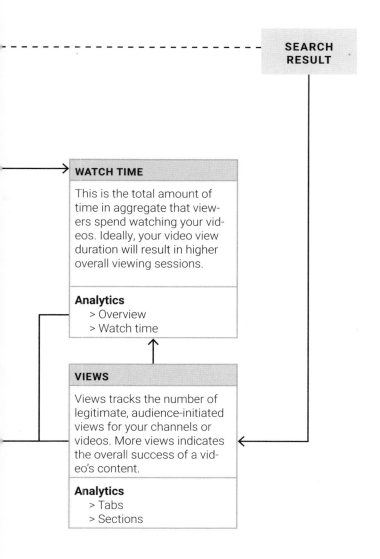

SEARCH RESULT

WATCH TIME

This is the total amount of time in aggregate that viewers spend watching your videos. Ideally, your video view duration will result in higher overall viewing sessions.

Analytics
> Overview
> Watch time

VIEWS

Views tracks the number of legitimate, audience-initiated views for your channels or videos. More views indicates the overall success of a video's content.

Analytics
> Tabs
> Sections

Along with a YouTube video checklist, I've also developed a YouTube *channel* checklist that includes detailed steps to optimize your channel for discovery, and accessibility. It also creates an opportunity for churches to engage with their YouTube subscribers and viewers.

YOUTUBE CHANNEL CHECKLIST:

1. **YouTube banner image.** This is the first impression people get of your church when they land on your YouTube channel, and as such, should reflect your church's mission and vision. I recommend your banner should include:

   • **A photo of your church building.** The goal of optimizing your YouTube content should be to connect with people who live within driving distance of your church. Having a photo of the front of the building will help make it feel more familiar the first time they attend an in-person service, because they've seen it online.

   An example of this style is North Point in Atlanta.

   • **A photo of your auditorium.** If you don't have a photo of your church building, another option is to use a photo of your auditorium. A photo of the main stage or kids and student environments give people an idea of what to expect if they visit your building in-person. An example of this style is Bethel Church in California.

   • **Content information.** While a lot of churches and ministries put their mission or vision on their YouTube banner, I usually advise churches to put channel content information, or online service times. For the casual viewer who is not aware of your church, this information is more helpful than your church mission. This can take various forms including the times for Sunday live streaming or how often new video content is uploaded to the channel.

Two good examples of this style are Elevation Church in North Carolina, and Village Church in British Columbia.

An example of a church incorporating all of these techniques is Life.Church in Oklahoma.

2. **YouTube About tab.** The YouTube "About" tab is where you can provide viewers with information about your church or ministry, location details such as your physical address, as well as links to your website, podcast, and social media channels. At the very least, if your church has a YouTube channel, I recommend making sure your "About" tab includes an email address, so people who watch your videos or visit your channel can engage with somebody from your church staff.

3. Welcome video. Every YouTube channel has a built-in welcome video that can be set to auto-roll whenever someone lands on the homepage. For churches, this welcome video should be between one and two minutes long, include information about your church, what sort of content can be found on your channel, and a call to action to subscribe to the channel, visit your website, or how they can connect with your church staff.

Here's a sample script for a YouTube welcome video:

Hey folks! Welcome to our YouTube channel.

I want to encourage you to stop right now and sub-scribe to the channel, so you can stay up to date with everything happening at our church. We would love for you to watch and comment on the videos, and share them with your family and friends.

We update this channel every week with new con-tent, so make sure you come back as often as you can, or click the bell icon at the bottom of a video so you get notified whenever we upload new content.

And if you'd like to find out more about our church, send us an email at info@churchname.com

3. Playlists. As mentioned earlier, a YouTube Playlist is a collection of videos on your YouTube channel that make content more accessible and discoverable. Playlists can also include a keyword description, providing another way for your content to rank.

4. Channel tags. Channel tags are words and phrases that highlight your channel and content. They are an essential part of making your channel discoverable. Channel tags can be added in YouTube Studio, and should include single words, phrases, and common misspellings. For example, when I was adding channel tags to North Point Community Church's YouTube channel, I made sure that I didn't use "north" as a single tag as this would potentially point to content on compasses. So, I made sure the tag phrases were "north point," "north point church," and "north point community church," but I also included "north pointe" as a common misspelling.

Now, it goes without saying that these are just some beginner steps to help YouTube your church, but even these may feel overwhelming if the YouTube world is new to you. That's okay. YouTube is a native language for most Millennials and Gen Z'ers. Recruiting help in making these changes is always a good idea. And keep in mind, a church that implements just these few steps should expect to see a substantial increase in video views, viewer retention, and new channel subscribers. When you give your content keyword titles to help answer your audience's search needs, upload videos with keyword metadata and tags to optimize discoverability, and provide engagement opportunities through pinned comments and descriptions with calls to action, you turn YouTube into an important tool in helping your church connect with your local community.

Skipping any of these steps will limit the impact of your message content on YouTube. For example, if you have your audience search and engagement worked out, but don't have discoverability, you're likely to get low overall views on your video because you're probably only reaching "insiders" when you upload. If you focus on engagement and discoverability, but not what your target audience is searching for, your videos are irrelevant to your community, so you will have low viewer retention. Likewise, if you prioritize search and discoverability, to the neglect of engagement, your content lacks authenticity and comes across as indifferent, leading to low engagement.

Here's a Venn diagram to explain an optimized YouTube video:

OPTIMIZED YOUTUBE CONTENT

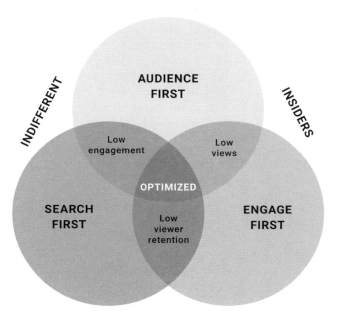

A fully optimized video on YouTube addresses the questions your audience is asking online, provides engagement opportunities, and is easily discoverable in a search. This video is more likely to get a high number of views, longer viewer retention, and will lead to ongoing conversations.

So, why should churches put time and resources into this process? Good question!

Isn't this just sideways energy that detracts from the mission of going into the world to preach the Gospel and make disciples? Nope. Let me explain.

According to pastor and author Jonathan "JP" Pokluda, YouTube is a fulfillment of Jesus' words that he would build his Church. In 2020,

JP—who is the lead pastor of Harris Creek Baptist Church in Waco, Texas, and author of two best-selling books, *Welcome to Adulting* and *Welcoming the Future Church*—saw so much potential in investing in a YouTube strategy that he hired a YouTuber to help him preach better and reach more people online.

"YouTube is just the next iteration of how Jesus' words in Matthew 16 are coming to fruition. His Church is prevailing over evil. It is another platform where His word bursts forth and pushes back darkness," JP told me in October 2021. "If the sermon is the mail, YouTube is the mailman. If the sermon is water, YouTube is another pipe to carry to foreign nations thirsty for truth."

I couldn't agree more with JP. And to take it one step further, optimizing your content on YouTube is the process of unclogging the pipe to ensure your video content is able to flow to as many people as possible! We can't afford to miss the opportunity. As a dad, I want to make sure that my three daughters have access to helpful, relevant answers to any questions about faith, hope, Jesus, and the Bible that they go online to ask.

The next step after that is to create multiple pipelines so that the streams of water your church is creating are able to reach even more people and attract new audiences! And that's what we're going to unpack next.

CHAPTER 09

REPURPOSE ON PURPOSE

"

While other rabbis and teachers now build a platform, Jesus built a pipeline, and his impact was inconceivably greater.

WILL MANCINI AND CORY HARTMAN,
FUTURE CHURCH: SEVEN LAWS OF REAL CHURCH GROWTH

EVERY CHURCH I'VE EVER BEEN part of dedicates a minimum of 30 minutes of their Sunday service to the sermon. According to Pew Research[60], this tracks. They analyzed almost 50,000 sermons between April and May 2019 in one of "the most exhaustive attempts to date to catalogue and analyze American religious sermons." The study found that the average length of a sermon was 37 minutes.

Now, compare that with the average length of a video on YouTube.

In 2014, the average length[61] of a YouTube video was four minutes and 20 seconds. In August 2021, the average length had increased to 11 minutes and 42 seconds[62]. A reason for the increase could be that in July 2020, Youtube introduced mid-roll ads for videos over eight minutes in length—meaning video creators could add more ad-breaks in their videos if the content ran over eight minutes. Prior to this, videos needed to be 10 minutes or longer to qualify for midroll ads.

Regardless of the reason, the point is the same. Church messages and sermon videos are more than triple the length of the average content on YouTube.

Now, you may be thinking that it's unfair to compare Sunday sermons to YouTube videos, since people will sit to watch a movie that's between 90 and 120 minutes, or binge-watch a series on Netflix that could be a dozen hours or more. But the difference here is that movies and Netflix content are made specifically for entertainment. I doubt there would be a pastor alive today who writes a sermon purely for entertainment value. And while yes, there is a lot of entertainment content on YouTube as well, remember, YouTube is the second biggest search engine in the world, which means people go there for information and answers. In this way, a lot of YouTube content acts more like a Sunday sermon than a Netflix series.

You may also be thinking the comparison to Youtube content and a Sunday sermon is unfair because people listen to long podcasts, which is also true. The top five podcasts in the U.S. in October 2021 range in length from 25-95 minutes. But the benefit of listening to a podcast is the ability to multitask. People listen to podcasts as they commute, work out, or clean their house—but most pastors want people's full attention when they preach. No one, as far as I've experienced, brings a treadmill to church with them in order to knock out a few miles while listening to their pastor preach! This makes the Sunday message different to these other forms of content that people regularly consume.

CONTENT THAT CONNECTS

It's easy for those of us in ministry to assume people simply can't wait to attend church on Sundays, but that's not reality. The length of the sermon is just one of the factors church leaders need to contend with in the postmodern world. Carey Nieuwhof says we're also contending with overarching anxiety[63]. "The average unchurched person doesn't lie awake on Saturday night wondering what you're going to preach on next." What actually keeps these people up is anxiety about their household bills and car payments. They lie awake wondering if their marriage will survive the current season, if their kids will be okay, and if anyone at work knows how much they are struggling to keep up. The average unchurched person is more concerned about their own physical and mental health than whether or not the pastor of the church down the road is starting a new message series.

If we want to engage with people in our community, then we have to realize that in-person church is not competing with online church, but rather *indifference* to church. That's why we need to make it as easy as possible for people to access and engage with our content.

> **If we want to engage with people in our community, then we have to realize that in-person church is not competing with online church, but rather *indifference* to church.**

Simply posting a 37-minute message video to YouTube is not the answer! If you think of people inviting their family and friends to watch your online services as a ladder, a Sunday sermon is usually the bottom rung on that ladder. But, when we ask people to watch a 37 minute message on a mobile device (Google reports that more than 70% of online video content is viewed on mobile devices[64]) we've made the lowest rung on the digital invitation ladder too high for many people to reach.

Making it easy for more people to engage with your church content online doesn't mean watering down or shortening the in-person message, but editing the online version of the message into easily digestible segments as part of the uploading process.

To make your content more shareable—and to encourage your church community to invite their unchurched friends to engage with your videos—requires a strategic plan to repurpose on purpose. You can strategically use short-form and micro-form content that will lead people to full messages, and then message series. When we repurpose content on purpose for the platforms and devices people use every day, we lower the bottom rung on the digital invitation ladder. This means providing content of varying lengths that are more consumable and act as lead magnets.

So, to be really clear, I'm not suggesting we replace 37 minutes of content with 11 minutes of content. I'm suggesting we *enhance* the original video by creating shorter segments edited from the 37 minutes (that are uploaded as separate videos) designed to ultimately lead people to the original full-length video.

This is repurposing your content on purpose.

For example, a long-form (37-minutes) LIVE message can be repurposed as:

- one or two short-form videos (4-7minutes) for YouTube, LinkedIn, Facebook, or Twitter
- a few micro-messages (30-90 seconds) for posting to YouTube and traditional social media platforms like Instagram, Facebook, and Twitter

The goal is to make it as easy as possible for people to take the next step in their faith journey. To do that, each step needs to be easy, obvious, and strategic. If you're ready to do this with your content, check out the pyramid below.

THE CONTENT PYRAMID

The process of repurposing on purpose starts with the foundational long-form content being captured LIVE in service on Sunday. This full-length, "long-form" message is distributed to various platforms like YouTube, on your church website as video on-demand, a sermon podcast, and maybe even uploaded directly to Facebook.

The next step is to edit this video to create "short-form" videos that are 4-8 minutes in length. These videos are distributed to social media channels and YouTube, with a clear call to action pointing to the full-length message and includes a link to the long-form, original message.

The final step in the process is to edit what I call "micro-content" from the message video, to be used as social media posts. This content is anywhere from 30-90 seconds for Instagram Reels, Instagram Stories, and YouTube Shorts, and up to two minutes for TikTok, Facebook, and LinkedIn. The process looks like an inverted pyramid.

REPURPOSE ON PURPOSE CONTENT STRATEGY

LONG-FORM CONTENT
35+ minute full message

The full message video from Sunday is distributed to **YouTube**, your church **website** as video-on-demand, and the audio is stripped for use as a **podcast**.

SHORT-FORM CONTENT
4–7 minute
highlight

A short-form edit of the message, featuring either a summary or single point, that is then distributed to **YouTube** with cards, end screens, and YouTube description pointing to the full message. This content is also suitable for **Facebook** and **Twitter** with links.

MICRO CONTENT
1–2 min
point

A single point or bottom line from the message is edited and distributed to **Instagram**, **IG Stories**, **TikTok**, **Twitter**, and **Facebook** with links to the short-form content as well as appropriate links to the full message.

An additional step of this "repurpose on purpose" process is to create quote graphics from the original message for social media platforms. These can be posted as either graphics to the Instagram grid, Twitter, and Facebook, or animated and posted as an Instagram Reel or TikTok video.

This is the model I've used since 2018, and it can work for you too—no matter the size of your church or your budget. In addition, even if the social media platforms change, the idea and purpose behind the structure doesn't.

Once you've posted the long-form message to YouTube, you use the YouTube end screen to direct people to the series playlist on your YouTube channel, and the video description to connect audiences with your website and social media platforms. You can also use YouTube cards to connect people with other messages in the series, or similar content.

Just about every church with a YouTube channel posts the message from their service, but only a few churches create 30-90 second "micro content" that is uploaded as YouTube Shorts. And even fewer do a "short form" version of the message that is anywhere from four to seven minutes.

The short form video is a key step in the digital invitation ladder. It's easy for people to share a 30 or 60-second video on social media, but the leap from one minute to 37 minutes is vast. That's why it's important to provide an intermediate step to bridge the gap between one and 37 minutes. These short form videos provide additional context to the message, and can be edited in a way that answers the specific questions people are asking in their zero moment of truth.

These short-form videos also create all-new content opportunities beyond those outlined above. For example, the short-form, four to seven minute videos can be used to create a midweek, short podcast in line with other podcasts such as Ted Talks Daily[65] which run between four and 12 minutes, TedX Shorts[66] which average between six to eight minutes, or NPR News Now[67] which is usually just five minutes. As always, these short podcasts would provide links to the full-length messages or message series.

A short form video could also be an important resource for small group ministries, giving group leaders a summary of the message to watch at the start of the group time to kick off discussion. And these videos can also be used as social media posts, recapping the previous Sunday, or promoting the coming Sunday services.

The goal is to make it as easy as possible for people to take the next step in their faith journey.

Let me add a quick side note here. Most churches I work with around the world typically use Monday mornings to post a "what you missed yesterday at church" video or graphic to social media. I'm not sure when or why this started, but it has always struck me as unusual. In the same way that unchurched people aren't spending Saturday nights wondering what will happen at your church on Sunday, they aren't waking up Monday morning wondering what they missed the day before at the church down the street they've never attended. Yet, we still post photos and videos to tell people "what an incredible Sunday we had," or how "yesterday was a great day."

I'm of the opinion that the better alternative is to post a short-form summary video of Sunday's message to social media on Friday or

Saturday afternoon in order to let people know what was discussed the previous week. When I was growing up, every Thursday night as I settled in for a new episode of *Battlestar Galactica*, the show would start with the voice-over, "Last week on *Battlestar Galactica* . . ." followed by a recap to remind

In this technological age, our potential influence hinges on our ability to learn a new skill, more than our budget to build a bigger building or increase the size of our staff.

me what happened on the previous episode. I think a pre-Sunday post like this would be far more helpful and relevant, and could entice people to come for the first time, or the first time in a long time. And for regular attendees, the post would act as a reminder of the series currently being preached.

Okay, back to repurposing.

The next step beyond these edited videos and graphic posts would be to use a service like Rev.com, Scribie or Otter.ai etc. to get a transcription of the message that could be edited and turned into a blog post. These posts, if properly optimized, would be another lead magnet to draw people to your church. You can also upload the transcript as a closed caption file to YouTube to serve people who are hard of hearing.

If a message could be properly repurposed in this manner, the end result could be 20 or more pieces of content made up of five or more tweet variations for testing with and without graphics or images, one or two quote graphics for use on Instagram, Facebook, and LinkedIn, two YouTube videos of varying lengths, a full-length message for your website or church app, a podcast episode, one micro-video for Instagram Reels, YouTube Shorts, and TikTok, and a blog post. It would also include Twitter posts made up of graphics, quotes, and videos, that I recommend scheduling three times on the first day the message goes live (3 for 1), twice a day for the first week the message is live (2 for 7), and twice a month for the following six months (2 for 6).

This can be visualized by the chart on the following page.

CONTENT DISTRIBUTION PLAN FOR
A METACHURCH STRATEGY

METACHURCH
DISCIPLESHIP
STRATEGY

The front door to your church
is in people's pocket

CONTENT
DISTRIBUTION

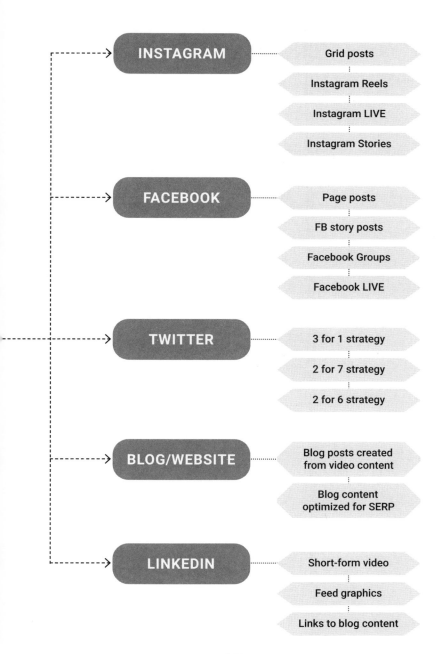

CHURCH WEEKLY CONTENT DISTRIBUTION PLAN

So how would all of this look across a week of social media and online posts at your church? Well, if a church was to create all of this extra content and distribute it across a week on multiple platforms, the plan could look like this.

SUNDAY AM	SUNDAY PM	MONDAY AM	TUESDAY AM
Sunday service live-stream	Sunday message to VOD website	Podcast of Sunday message content	Short-form of Sunday message content
	Message only posted to YouTube channel	I recommend using a platform that allows geo-tagged intros as part of the church's digital assimilation process.	This includes 4–7 minutes posted to YouTube and social media in appropriate formats.
	This should follow custom YouTube SOPs to optimize reach and engagement.	Blog version of Sunday message with small group questions	
		This could leverage a transcription service and be formatted for small group leaders.	

This is a distribution plan based on weekly church content opportunities. This plan provides multiple touch points each week across multiple channels and platforms, but does not currently include a church email strategy. Each step needs to have SOPs developed by the church social media team and needs to be assessed according to the church's core values.

WEDNESDAY	THURSDAY AM	FRIDAY	SATURDAY
Midweek podcast	**Family ministries video content**	**Podcast of family ministries content**	**Micro-message version of Sunday message content**
This could be a Bible study, a leadership message, or a message based off a Sunday's sermon.	This should be designed to resource parents so they can be equipped to disciple their children.		This is a 60–90 second recap of Sunday's message and acts as promo for Sunday by recapping the previous week's message.
		Blog of family ministries content	
This should be a short-form podcast with CTAs connecting the audience to other church content.		This would be cleaned up and edited to suit a written format.	This would be posted to all social media channels.

This repurposing and distribution strategy lowers the bottom rung on the digital invitation ladder by giving people access to your church's content at times and on platforms that are suited for the average person's needs. When people can engage with your church's messages and share your content in ways that integrate with their lifestyle, you create opportunities to find new audiences.

And let me add one more thing. You can apply this strategy to your message archive as well.

My oldest daughter watches three sitcoms on rotation: *The Office*, *Brooklyn Nine-Nine,* and *Parks and Recreation*. Almost every time I see her watching videos on her iPad, she's watching one of these sitcoms. Yes, she's seen every episode of every series multiple times, yet she still watches them, and still laughs. She doesn't care at all that *Brooklyn Nine-Nine* was first released in September 2013, that *Parks and Recreation* started in April 2009, or that the first episode of *The Office* aired in the U.S. in March 2005! It's the same with your church content.

People don't care that a message is old, they care that it's relevant. That message you preached on hope more than a year ago is still relevant because hope is still relevant. The message series from three summers ago about how to survive toxic relationships is just as important today as the day you wrote it.

For decades, churches have been content creating machines. Every single week we create sermon series, student messages, classes and courses, webinars, staff talks, bulletins, baptism videos, social media posts, and kids content. Creating content is something the modern Church does extremely well. What we don't do well is *distribute* that content.

Now, I totally understand it may feel overwhelming to begin to implement all of these repurposing on purpose steps. But the best news is that these tools are at the fingertips of every church leader. They are equally available to all of us, no matter our church size, staff, or budget. In other words, in this technological age, our potential influence hinges on our ability to learn a new skill, more than our budget to build a bigger building or increase the size of our staff. You have more control than you think. And while it can all feel overwhelming, more than anything, you should feel empowered. Why? Because the ability to engage with people in your local community, and give them the content they need right when and how they need it, rests with you.

CHAPTER 10
WHAT IS YOUR SOCIAL MEDIA FOR?

"

A social media plan focuses on getting people to the building for a couple of hours every weekend, whereas a social ministry strategy focuses on how to help them grow in their faith through social technology after they leave. You need both, and if you focus only on a social media plan, you will build an audience while stopping short of building disciples.

NONA JONES, *FROM SOCIAL MEDIA TO SOCIAL MINISTRY: A GUIDE TO DIGITAL DISCIPLESHIP*

THE LARGEST CHURCH I WAS ever part of in Australia had about 600 people in attendance. Just before moving with my family to the U.S. in 2008 to become an online pastor, my wife and I had helped grow a church from 110 to 150 people. So you can imagine the culture shock we experienced when we joined the staff at North Point Ministries, a church that pre-COVID-19 was averaging about 40,000 people attending every Sunday at seven Atlanta-area locations. In fact, for the whole time we were part of North Point, 2013 to 2020, our church was consistently in the top three largest churches in the U.S.

My role as the social media pastor at North Point was to look after the people who connected with our church digitally through social media, websites and apps, podcasts, and YouTube. Whenever I would talk to pastors and church leaders about my role at North Point, one of the first two questions they always asked was how many people attended the church.

My answer to the numbers question always got a reaction as people wrapped their heads around the overwhelming size of North Point's influence. And it *was* impressive. But what I always found even more amazing was knowing that those 40,000 people in physical attendance didn't represent even half of the engagement on our digital platforms. During the time I was at North Point, four times that number accessed our content via podcast every month, twice the number of physical attendees watched our services online or through video on-demand from our website or church app, and if you added all the people who followed our collective churches on Instagram, Facebook, and Twitter, there were over a million people connecting with our church via social media.

We needed to stop using social media as a megaphone to broadcast our content, and instead, start using it as a telephone to build our community.

That was overwhelming.

But I've always believed that numbers only matter because people count, and each of those followers represented a person who had questions, hopes, dreams, careers, bills to pay, opinions, errands to run, and family and friends to care for. I understood that social media was not just the front door of our church for these people, it was also the way many of them connected with us. It's for this reason that church social media took on a whole new purpose for me.

As the person overseeing North Point's social media strategy, I felt responsible for ensuring that we got the most out of every social media channel, so I kept a list of all the social media platforms we used and the tools they offered, as well as the social media opportunities we had available that we weren't using yet. This list was constantly changing as platforms introduced new features, or new, alternative channels were started. When I moved back to Australia at the end of 2020, here's what this running list looked like:

SOCIAL MEDIA CONTENT FOR A METACHURCH STRATEGY

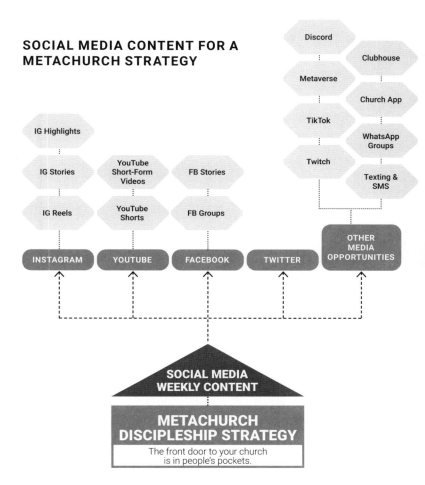

Given my role, I felt responsible for shepherding the people who connected with us online, so I saw social media as a tool for our church to live out Ephesians 4:12. Whether it was posting a photo to Instagram, producing a Facebook LIVE, or sending out a tweet, everything we posted was a chance *"to equip the saints for the work of ministry, for building up the body of Christ,"* (Ephesians 4:12 ESV). But to do this, we needed to stop using social media as a megaphone to broadcast our content, and instead, start using it as a telephone to build our community.

This shift in approach changed everything. I started to view social media at all of our churches through a different lens. I adopted the philosophy that building community on social media is more important than broadcasting content. Or, as my mate Beau Coffron, social media director at Life.Church says, "Social media isn't a task to be finished, it's an opportunity for ministry." Beau's point is that every social media post is an opportunity to reach, engage with, and encourage another person. "Our social media channels shouldn't be a billboard that people drive by. They should be a coffee shop that people hang out in."

When we leverage social media with building community in mind, it becomes an invaluable part of a MetaChurch strategy because our church social media becomes far more personal and purposeful. But this shift requires intentionality.

POSTS WITH PURPOSE

Social media is a key part of a MetaChurch model, or any church's strategy, when *every post has a purpose*. To this end, everything a church posts to social media should fall into one of three categories:

1. Awareness
2. Loyalty
3. Advocacy

Posts that fall into the "Awareness" category are those that are specifically designed to make people in your town or city aware of your church. In church world, we like to believe that everyone in our city or town is aware of our church name and community. But as discussed in the last chapter, most unchurched people are indifferent to the Church. So, you need to make them aware of your church community.

A few ways you can do this include:

- Leverage local hashtags so you can join local conversations.
- Create posts that celebrate causes, schools, first responders, teachers, businesses, etc. in your community.
- Shout out local businesses (cafés, restaurants, printers, etc.) and tag them in a social media post.
- Highlight and celebrate local charity organizations.

An example of a community awareness post could be using Twitter's geographic hashtag search. For example, you can search the hashtag "MovingDay" within a 10 mile radius of your church building to find and welcome new residents who have moved to the area.

A couple of years ago, I was searching the hashtag, "IHateMondays," when I found a tweet from a local couple who had lost their dog. Using the church account, I quoted the couple's tweet and asked our church family to contact the owners if they saw the dog. A few days later, the couple found their dog, and tweeted at our church to thank us for our help. This was a couple who had never set foot inside our church building, but were now thanking our church community for helping them in their moment of need.

Building community on social media is more important than broadcasting content.

"Loyalty" posts are any content that is specifically for "insiders" at your church. These posts are designed to deepen the connection between people who are already part of your church community and your church staff. Posts in this category would include Facebook and Instagram lives, church event invitations, celebrations and highlights, and anything posted to a church Facebook Group.

Finally, posts that fit in the "Advocacy" category are those that are purposefully designed for church "insiders" to share on their own social media channels to create awareness of your church in the local community. These posts would include new message series promotions, short-form videos edited from the Sunday message (see chapter 9), and posts celebrating local and national holidays. The idea is to create content that allows people to invite their family and friends to church, and to share their faith (more about this in chapter 15).

If you really want to go the extra mile with advocacy posts, consider creating a website where people can download pre-made content to share on their own social media accounts. We did this at North Point for our Easter services, providing artwork in various sizes for all platforms, even including suggested captions to make it even easier for people to share. If you'd like to check out what this looks like, go to easterwithus.com/share.

Here's a breakdown of the three posting categories and some ideas for posts that fall into each. Following this strategy will ensure everything you post to social media has a specific purpose.

SOCIAL MEDIA POSTING CATEGORIES

AWARENESS (40%)	LOYALTY (40%)	ADVOCACY (20%)
Social media posts that are specifically designed to create awareness of your church throughout the local community.	Content posted for "insiders" to deepen the connections with people who are part of your church community.	Posts designed for current "insiders" to share on their platforms, to create awareness of your church in the local community.
Short-form video content from Sunday's message.	Church event or class invitations and reminders.	New message series promotional content.
Posts that celebrate local community events & holidays.	Message preview posts on Fridays or Saturdays.	Short-form videos edited from the Sunday messages.
Posts calling out local schools and local first responders	Facebook & Instagram LIVE Bible study videos.	Links to the church's YouTube channel and video content.
Posts that specifically celebrate local businesses.	Facebook Groups linked to from the main church page.	Quote graphics from Sunday & special event messages.
Using local hashtags to join in on local conversations.	Church event celebration & highlight posts.	Posts celebrating local & national holidays.

The percentage next to each section is a suggestion for how often posts should be used from each category. Awareness posts should make up 40% of your church social media posts because the Church should be an outward facing entity that is an active part of the local community. Forty percent should be Loyalty posts because the Church should give equal resources to making disciples as it does to going into all the world. And the 20% should be Advocacy posts to equip the people already connected with your church to invite their family and friends. These percentages will change based on ministry seasons throughout the year, with Christmas and Easter, for example, being times when Advocacy posts encourage your church community to invite their family and friends to specific services or series.

If you're not sure where to get started, try this. Here's a month's worth of social media post suggestions pulled from each category in the corresponding post percentage.

SAMPLE MONTH OF SOCIAL MEDIA POSTS

WEEK 1	WEEK 2	WEEK 3	WEEK 4
Ask people to nominate their favorite local coffee shop.	Cheer on other churches in your local community.	Post info for restaurants near your church.	Tell your church how they can help the local aged community.
Cheer on the fire fighters in your local community.	Ask people how you can pray for their week.	Post photos of your church serving the community.	Provide a full week of recipe ideas for parents.
Give parents a question to ask their kids after school.	Post 5 things Christians can do to love their neighbors.	Stream 60-mins of kids' content so parents can talk to each other.	Post encourage-ment for local medical workers.
Go live on a platform and ask people how you can pray for them.	Promote mental health resources in your community.	Spend the day commenting on local businesses' social media.	Post non-church inspirational quotes on perseverance.
Post a stress-re-lieving Spotify or Apple Music playlist.	Promote date night ideas for couples in the community.	Promote a non-church local com-munity Facebook group.	Post support for your local community sports teams.
Post 10 family-friendly outing ideas in your community.	Post support for your local ambu-lance services.	Tell people how they can pray for local teachers.	Share a series of helpful non-church podcasts.
List 10 local non-church charities where people can volunteer.	Provide details of local chari-ties people can support.	Promote local AA and rehab resources and meetings.	Encourage your church people to support local businesses.

ONE WEEK OF SOCIAL MEDIA POST IDEAS FOR CHURCHES OF ANY SIZE

SUNDAY AM	SUNDAY PM	MONDAY	TUESDAY	WEDNESDAY AM
Link to your online service or YouTube Use this to invite people to watch the service online.	**Tweet a quote from Sunday's message**	**Tweet with encouraging Bible verse and image from unsplash.com**	**Motivational quote from well-known leader or author**	**Tweet support for a local business**
Instagram promo of your service Instead of randomly inviting people, tell them exactly what they will learn if they attend or watch the service. EG: *"Today we will show you 5 things you can do to find peace in hard times."*	**Quote graphic from Sunday's message** Make sure you include a question mark in the caption to encourage engagement. EG: *"How will you apply today's message at home or work this week?"*	**Post cheering on a local school and their teaching staff** Make sure you tag the schools you mention.	**Post highlighting a church volunteer of the week**	**Facebook LIVE with 5-minute Bible devotion based on current series**
Poll on IG Story How are you coping with local lockdowns?		**Ask people how you can pray for them this coming week** Make sure everyone who leaves a comment gets a response. Set aside time at the end of your day to respond to everyone.		**Instagram LIVE where you pray for people**
Post information letting parents know what is happening in your family ministry services today				**Short YouTube LIVE asking people for prayer requests**
Livestream service to YouTube LIVE If you can only stream to one platform, YouTube will give you the best quality views without audio being cut during worship.			These live-streams only need to be 5 minutes but give you a chance to regularly connect with your church community.	

And if you're wondering what this might look like across a week's worth of posts at your church, along with some of the repurpose on purpose suggestions I made in the previous chapter, here's an example.

WEDNESDAY PM	THURSDAY	FRIDAY AM	FRIDAY PM	SATURDAY
Tweet support for a local business	Tweet a suggested reading list from your staff	Tweet Bible verse about rest	Cheer on local emergency workers and tag departments	Tweet preview of Sunday's message topic/content
Shout out a local business or service the church uses or frequents	IG Story quote from Sunday's message	Friday night at home suggestions in an IG carousel post	Family friendly weekend suggestion in your town	Give a preview of what Sunday's message topic will be
	Shout out a local business or service the church uses or frequents	Post cheering on local school and their teaching staff		Pre-scheduled post highlighting a family activity in your local community
		Make sure you tag the schools you mention.		

Posts on Friday & Saturday should be prescheduled in advance so you and your staff can have two days off social media.

KEY	TWITTER	INSTAGRAM	FACEBOOK	YOUTUBE

A social media schedule like this goes beyond just one-way, mega-phone communication about church events or an out-of-context Bible verse. This is a posting schedule that provides opportunities for discipleship, encouragement, and connection. And now, more than ever before, *people need connection*.

PERSONAL CONNECTIONS

I think most of us would agree that while we live in a world that is more connected than ever before, more people are experiencing isolation than at any time in history. In July 2021, the European Commission's science and knowledge service[68] released data showing that one in four people in Europe felt lonely during the pandemic. In America, three in five people[69] were lonely according to a 2020 survey[70] conducted by U.S. health insurer Cigna[71], and in Australia this number was at one in two[72] according to 2021 figures[73] reported by Australian Institute of Health and Welfare[74].

According to the Cigna research, Gen Z is the most isolated generation with 79% of participants in this category reporting they feel lonely. This means that statistically, the generation that has grown up with and is most active on social media, feels the most lonely. Gen Z-ers may have 10,000 followers, but they feel like they have no friends—not even in the church!

In February 2021[75], Springtide Research Institute surveyed 2500 mem-bers[76] of Generation Z (ages 13 to 25) and revealed that nine out of 10 young people didn't hear from a faith leader during the pandemic. Let that sink in. Only 10% of the young people surveyed said a pastor or church staff member had checked in to see how they were doing.

I asked Springtide to break down their research by people affiliated with church (churchgoers) and non-affiliated, and they shared that of the 1685 respondents of the study who were affiliated with a church, 224—which is just 13%—said they heard from a faith leader. And by "faith leader," they meant "someone with a position of leadership and influence in a faith group or religious group." This means that 87% of people affiliated with a church did not hear from a "faith leader." Springtide's executive director, Josh Packard, said there's "a whole lot of things" the Church has missed. "We were hearing lots of news stories about religious leaders scrambling to put services online," Packard said. "And at the same time, we're hearing from young people that nobody was really checking in on them, especially religious leaders."

"This research really rattled me," Kara Powell, Executive Director of Fuller Youth Institute and associate professor of Youth and Family Ministry, told me after reading the research. "These teenagers experience loneliness because they want a sense of belonging and to connect with other humans. This is a divine reminder that we need to prayerfully and thoughtfully build relationships with young people."

To help them, we need to make social media more personal—so we can create deeper connections in our churches and in the local communities where God has called us to serve. We have to decide whether or not we want our social media channels to be all about us and what we're doing, or reaching, serving, encouraging, and discipling others. The point of social media is to be "social"—to make connections. It's not called "promotion media"! This technology gives us the chance to engage with a generation that is as lonely as any generation before it.

As church leaders, we have the chance to use social media for so much more than promoting our own events. We can use it to engage people in real and authentic connections. Because the truth is, if we don't get this right with our social media channels, we are missing more than an opportunity to connect with people. We are missing an opportunity to work at eliminating the problem of loneliness and isolation these very tools can perpetuate. We don't want to be part of the problem. And we don't have to be. Done well, we can offer a solution. Done with purpose, we can offer hope.

CHAPTER 11

PREACH LIKE A YOUTUBER

"

*Christian communicators must show that
we remember (or at least understand) very
well what it is like not to believe.*

TIM KELLER, *PREACHING: COMMUNICATING
FAITH IN AN AGE OF SKEPTICISM*

I ONCE PLAYED GUITAR for Richie Sambora.

For those under 40, Richie Sambora is the guitar hero from legendary
rock band Bon Jovi, and the man responsible for the epic guitar riffs
in classic songs like "Living on a Prayer," "You Give Love a Bad Name,"
and "Wanted Dead or Alive." (And if you don't know those songs, close
this book right now, and go listen to them. I will wait.)

Back to the story. When I was in my mid-20s, I won a radio competition
in Melbourne, Australia to meet Richie and receive a guitar lesson from
him. When the lesson got underway, he asked me to play something
so he could assess my ability level. In my nervousness, the only thing
I could think of playing was the opening lick of "Wanted Dead or Alive."
That's right, I chose to play *checks notes* Richie Sambora's most
famous guitar lick *in front of Richie Sambora!* Halfway through the
lick, it dawned on me what I was doing, and if I didn't already have
both hands on my guitar, I would have slapped myself.

That said . . . Richie said I crushed the lick.

But the nerves I felt that day as I played guitar in front of my favorite guitar player, was nothing compared to how I felt the first time I preached at North Point in front of Andy Stanley.

When I was first asked to speak on a Sunday at North Point, I was excited. I knew that the service production team and Andy would want to go over my content to make it better, and I would get a crash course in preaching from one of the best, most respected, and influential communicators in the world. In the week leading up to my message, Andy provided some notes, and his team helped restructure part of my message to make it flow better. I was thrilled to get such comprehensive feedback and it made that message one of the best I'd ever preached.

But honestly, if I had my time over, the message I preached that day is not the message I'd preach now with what I've learned from YouTube content creators.

My message that day ran about 35 minutes, and included a series of slides with Bible text and bottom lines, photos of my family and of me in my TV reporter days, and I even played a high-pitched sound that only people under the age of 20 could hear (really). I was happy with my message. But if I had my time over again, I would preach that message completely differently.

I would keep all of the main points, the same biblical text, and even the high-pitched sound. But I would cut 15 minutes from the runtime, and change the way I introduced the topic in the opening two minutes. I would make these changes for one reason: watching YouTubers has changed the way I preach. (I'd also tell myself to get out of my head and quit worrying about what Andy was thinking, and instead just focus on connecting with the audience. But that's beside the point.)

PREACHING TO A CAMERA

Watching YouTubers has made me more clear and concise, more aware of my audience's attention span, and more cognizant of whether I am answering real questions about life, faith, and the text. YouTubers taught me the same thing that millions of pastors needed a global pandemic to learn: preaching to a video is different than preaching to an audience. Kenny Jahng agrees, saying, "If you are an amazing preacher behind the pulpit, it doesn't mean you're an amazing preacher in front of the camera." He's right!

When you're preaching to a camera, audience retention and engagement needs to be considered in a totally different way. That's why I encourage pastors to preach like a YouTuber, because YouTubers are masters at connecting with people via video, and they use a number of different tips and tricks that translate directly to live preaching.

> **Preaching to a video is different than preaching to an audience.**

So, whether you're the main speaker at your church, a volunteer or itinerant communicator, a children's or youth speaker, or someone who programs the church services, here are a few tips on how you can optimize your online and pre-recorded messages by preaching like a YouTuber. And it starts with a H.O.T. intro.

H stands for "hook." The hook is the thing that makes people want to listen to your message. When it comes to preaching, I've found that the best hook is to explain the burning question, issue, tension, or concern that your message answers for your audience. When I first started preaching messages, I was taught to start with an engaging story. But over the years, I've come to realize that the best way to hook people right from the start is to explain the topic of your message and why it's relevant. Some examples of what this may look like in church are:

- "Have you ever wanted to know what the purpose of your life is?"
- "The Bible can be so complicated, right? So how do you get the most out of it?"
- "We all have difficult people in our lives, so what is the best way to deal with them?

I don't always open a message with a question or statement like this— especially if I'm speaking at a new church or conference setting where I need to introduce myself and establish some credibility with the audience. But I usually plant a hook like this somewhere in the first few minutes of a message.

O stands for outcome. This is where you tell your audience exactly how they will benefit from your talk by sharing the outcome of the message right at the start. Now, it may sound counterintuitive to let people know the thing you want them to take away from the sermon, but by doing so, you let them know why they need to stay engaged for the entire message. You're basically giving away your preferred outcome for the audience right at the start. You are saving the *how* for later in the message, but you are telling the audience the *what* right away. You're letting them know that if they stick around, *this* is what they'll leave with. For example:

- "Now, in this message, I'm going to show you the simple life hack that is guaranteed to help you worry less!"
- "By the end of my message, I'm going to share with you the three things you can do today to make next year slightly better."
- "Today, I'm going to give you the secret to avoid being the person people think of when they think of mean people."

Again, this is a technique I use every time I preach or give a message, whether it's in-person or online, for a conference, webinar, or a presentation on Zoom. I've found that it streamlines my message and narrows my focus, because to explain the outcome I have to *know* the outcome myself!

T stands for transition. This is basically giving a verbal instruction or visual clue to let the audience know you're moving into the main content of the message. In my experience, the best speakers are the ones with the best transitions—those who can move their audience seamlessly from one section to the next. That's why I recommend a tight, scripted transition—otherwise it's easy to end up rambling and losing people. For example:

- "I'll start by asking you a question I already know the answer to . . ."
- "To do this, I want to tell you about the time my family and I . . ."
- "And today, I brought two friends with me to discuss how they . . ."

That's the HOT intro, and now that I've explained it, you won't be able to unsee it when you're next watching a YouTube video.

Once I transition into the bulk of my message, I like to ensure I'm building pattern interruptions into my message. Pattern interruptions are a sales and marketing technique that, according to a *Forbes* article[77] in July 2020 titled "The Science Behind Pattern Interruptions," are, "an extremely effective technique in sales that can change behaviors, assumptions, opinions and decisions in an instant, as it pushes people to not rely on their go-to responses." They are specifically designed to attract engagement and draw out the desired outcome. In a video message, the most important desired outcome is the viewer's attention.

YouTubers understand the importance of pattern interruptions when it comes to maintaining a viewer's attention in their videos—that's why you'll see the best YouTubers using things like b-roll, cutaways, slash-cams, slides, or jump cuts to break up the visual vanilla of a person standing in front of a camera speaking. A pattern interruption is any visual change that re-focuses the audience's attention. When I am preaching online or in a pre-recorded message, the pattern interruptions I use most often are jump cuts and full screen slides.

A jump cut is when a single camera shot is edited to make the person speaking appear closer to the camera than the previous shot. The idea of a jump cut is not to create a seamless transition between two separate shots, but to draw a comparison between the first and second shots. This works by breaking up the single shot, while also allowing you to emphasize specific points as needed.

The great thing about a simple jump cut like this is that it doesn't require any extra camera equipment or time shooting additional footage. I take the single shot I've recorded and increase the size of the shot so it appears to jump closer.

Here is an example of a single shot jump cut that I use in most of my online and pre-recorded video messages.

Shot one is wide and looks like this:

While shot two is actually the same shot, but blown up to 135%:

On average, I place cuts like these in my vision every 8-20 seconds depending on the topic and length of the video. I often use them in between sentences, but will also add them mid sentence if the section of the video is especially long.

Full-screen slides are another way I break up the vision of my online content. While a lot of churches use lower thirds for slides during a message, a full-screen slide is an easy way to introduce a pattern interruption.

142

Now, I'm sure almost every pastor understands using slides in a message—usually for things like Bible verses—but when it comes to video, how and when you use slides is as important as what you put on the slides. My thinking around this was shaped as much by YouTubers as it was by TED Talks.

In his 2014 book *Talk Like Ted: The 9 Public-Speaking Secrets of the World's Top Minds*, author Carmine Gallo writes, "when it comes to the brain's ability to pay attention to a lecture, conversation, or presentation, it is simply incapable of paying equal attention to multiple items."[78] Which is why Gallo argues that when we use slides, we should use as few words as possible, so people don't have to make a choice to either listen to the message or read the slide.

This is as important at an in-person service as it is at an online service.

"Think about it," Gallo writes. "Aren't we adding an impossible load on our audience when we ask them to listen intently to our words and read a lengthy PowerPoint slide at the same time?" So, he suggests each slide in a presentation be, at a maximum, no more than 40 words. "The average PowerPoint slide has 40 words. It's nearly impossible to find one slide in a TED presentation that contains anywhere near 40 words, and these presentations are considered among the best in the world."

This means splitting up long passages of Scripture into smaller chunks and building them over multiple slides, thus creating more pattern interruptions to maintain the audience's attention. This is a technique I've used in every in-person and online talk I've given since 2018. I've also found that separating long passages of Scripture this way allows me to draw out key words or phrases as the slides build. We often read the Bible like we're reading a recipe book—just a list of instructions to follow. But it's SO much more than that! It's a rich story that is full of complex characters, love interests, espionage, betrayal, redemption, and restoration; but it will also give insight to living, answers the questions most of us are asking, and provides hope! While we've got this great text that is alive and compelling, we need to bring it to life for modern day audiences. We need to preach the Bible in a way that makes people want to know more, want to come back to hear more, or want to read it for themselves!

Splitting up long passages of Scripture across multiple slides is a reminder for me to build energy or unpack the tension already baked into the text.

Another technique I use I learned from Andy. Anyone who has seen Andy preach at church or a conference in the past 10 years knows he has a preference for minimalist slides—white text on a black background. The only addition Andy teaches North Point speakers to use is to highlight any key words on a slide in yellow font. I've been using this technique for every message since 2014.

Here are a couple of examples of the sort of slides I use when I am preaching—whether in a physical space or cyberspace:

"A man was going down from Jerusalem to Jericho, when he was attacked by robbers."

Luke 10:30

Your neighbor is not just
the people who are like you,
but people who are nothing like you!

But jump cuts and full screen slides are not the only ways to create pattern interruptions. B-roll, slash cams, multiple camera angles, and cutaways are other options to help break up your vision to make it more engaging. During the COVID-19 lockdowns, I saw many churches shoot their online messages on-location—whether it was the pastor's living room or back porch, the lobby of the church, or a separate outdoor location that was congruent with the message. Harris Creek Baptist Church in Waco, Texas did this really well.

"An online experience must be engaging," Harris Creek lead pastor Jonathan "JP" Pokluda told me. "Historically, the online service was an unedited livestream or replay. But if it's only online, we decided to record early, in unusual places, using the setting to our advantage. At Easter, for example, we recorded in a cemetery. One Sunday we recorded at sunset by the lake. We were no longer constrained by Sunday morning."

When I asked JP why he decided to make these changes, his answer was personal. "My kids were restless and yawning while watching me on the TV, and I was usually talking about them!" JP said. "However, they are glued to their favorite YouTuber. He was making sculptures out of skittles and cutting watermelons with samurai swords, and my kids couldn't get enough of it. So as a church leadership, we started asking how we could make our messages more engaging."

Another area that JP addressed while answering this question was how long to make his messages online. "I think there is something about the length of messages right now. You're not going to want to watch something on a screen for as long as you do in-person."

As I mentioned in chapter 9, the average length of a sermon in the U.S. is 37 minutes, while the average length of a YouTube video is 11 minutes and 42 seconds. As I outlined in that chapter, I am not advocating that church messages be capped at 12 minutes, but I am suggesting that a change in format may require a change in method. Now, I know that even the suggestion of shortening the length of a sermon will cause some readers to see red. I'm sure some of you are already typing up your emails or tweets to me with your Bible open to Acts 20:9 which tells the story of Paul preaching so long that a dude fell asleep in a window ledge and fell to his death.

While Paul may have been a lengthy orator, one of the first messages Jesus gave in a synagogue was recorded as being just eight words long (depending on your translation).

> *"Today this Scripture is fulfilled in your hearing."*
> LUKE 4:21 NIV

That's it. That was his message.

A sermon does not have to be 30+ minutes in order to be "valid." Regardless of how long you think you *need* to preach to get your point across, you also need to understand how people in the digital age are absorbing content in their cultural context.

Let's be honest, none of us wants someone in our congregation to nod off and fall to their death during our message. Right?

One final tip about on-line preaching. And be warned, this one might be the most uncomfortable. If you want to improve, you need to watch the video of yourself communicating and take notes on what you can do better. Now, I get it. Watching yourself on video can be a painful, cringe-worthy event. But, that's actually the point. You will notice every single mistake, every verbal tic, every hand gesture, or lack thereof. And noticing those moments is the only way you'll learn what it's like to be on the other side of you.

I remember Andy telling a group of communicators at North Point the story of how, as a young preacher, he would get the cassette tapes of his messages and drive around Atlanta listening to them in his car. He explained that this was one of the best things he ever did to improve his public speaking. This is a step many pastors around the world have learned from Andy, but Carey Nieuwhof has added another degree of difficulty to this torturous venture. "If you're really brave—which you should be—get others to evaluate you and give you tips," he recommends. "Pain can be a great teacher. If you can't stand to watch yourself on video, why would anyone else watch you?"

While this chapter was about the messages at your church, remember that's just one aspect of making your online services more engaging. We can't just stop there.

We have to continually ask how we can make our entire service more engaging, creating greater opportunities to connect with people and encouraging them to connect in-person. If you're ready, turn the page and let's dig in.

CHAPTER 12

THE "PERFECT" ONLINE SERVICE

❝❝

The perfect church service would be one we were almost unaware of. Our attention would have been on God.

C.S. LEWIS, *LETTERS TO MALCOLM: CHIEFLY ON PRAYER*

IN MARCH OF 2020, MUCH of the world shut down due to the start of the COVID-19 pandemic. And like many of you, all of North Point's normally scheduled in-person services were sent online. For us, this wasn't too much of a change because when the pandemic started, North Point had already been streaming its services online for close to a decade. In fact, we were known to have higher viewer retention rates than other churches our size.

But in April 2020 all of that had changed.

Our normally high online viewer retention had dropped more than 20% in just over a month. And everyone was asking why.

Here was our path to discovery:

> **Step one:** Consult Google analytics.
> **Step two:** Check your YouTube Studio data.

The results were conclusive—people were not watching the musical worship section of our online services. They were either coming into the online service late so they could just watch Andy's message, or they were fast-forwarding past the three worship songs at the beginning of our video-on-demand services for the same reason. In fact, YouTube analytics showed a dramatic drop in viewers at the beginning of each service when the music started, followed by an equally dramatic spike in viewers when the message started.

We had our reason. We might not have liked it. But the data didn't lie.

If we wanted viewers to engage, we needed to start with the message, cut back on music (something that unsettled me as a musician and member of the North Point worship team) and move it to the end of the online stream. This solution happened to be the exact opposite of how we programmed for in-person services.

We always started our services with worship so people who arrived late wouldn't miss any of the message. But now, with all of our services online, we needed to switch things up. Thankfully, since everything was pre-recorded for the pandemic, we could easily move elements around to test out our theory.

As it turned out, the very next Sunday, our online service started with the normal online-stinger (a short 3-8 second video clip with music that is designed to call the audience's attention to the screen. If you've ever watched ESPN SportsCentre, you've seen a stinger), which was immediately followed by the welcome and message. After the closing prayer, the camera faded to black and the musical worship section started. The team played one song and the service was done in 45 minutes.

And guess what? Google and YouTube analytics gave us the data we were hoping for: Our viewer retention rate was back above 70% at almost all of our locations.

TIME TO CHANGE

That was when my philosophy about online service programming changed. I realized two things needed to happen in the "traditional" church online service programming model, moving beyond just a straight broadcast of the physical service.

1. The length of the online service needed to change.

When we adopted this strategy at North Point, our viewer retention rate literally increased overnight. And North Point is not an isolated case. When I discussed online services with Jonathan "JP" Pokluda, lead pastor of Harris Creek Baptist Church in Waco, Texas, he said they made a similar decision to shorten the overall time frame of their services during the pandemic.

"During the shutdown I taught for a shorter period of time," JP told me. "We decided to experiment and do anything we could do to keep people engaged in the Bible—short of Skittles sculptures and samurai swords!" JP explained that his team continued to make changes to their traditional model based on their online data, and they don't plan to stop now that their building has opened up. "Today, we are continuing to reevaluate everything and plan to make some hires to help us own this area [of online streaming]. While we will soon be maxed out on space over three services, we know even more people will be 'attending' from somewhere else online."

2. Streaming music during online services needed to stop.

This is a little more controversial, so let me explain.

Musical worship is one of the hardest things to get right in an online live stream. I mean, there's a reason why Broadway shows are rarely broadcasted online or on TV, preferring for people to experience a musical in-person. And when a Broadway show does take the plunge into recording a version of the performance, it's not done live in one take as most church worship sets are. Take the Disney+ version of Lin-Manuel Miranda's hit musical *Hamilton* for example. According to screenrant.com[79], the show took more than $12.5 million USD to produce, and required professional singers to have three separate stage productions filmed and edited together to create the movie.

And still, church leaders try to stream live music online every week with volunteer singers and production teams. While we're all aiming for the same high-level of music as Disney+, there's a few reasons why it's so hard to do well.

First, the live, in-the-room environment is far more forgiving of your worship team vocalists. A slightly off-pitch note is missed in the room when it is combined with the hundreds of other voices alongside it. But online, any pitch errors are a lot more obvious. Just ask any musician who has listened back to a live recording of themselves.

Second, mixing live music for online viewing is hard. To make the live music stream the highest quality at North Point, we had a pur-pose-built online mixing studio that would take the feed from in the room and mix it down for online speakers. This meant making the music sound high quality on whichever device people were watching through, whether it was smart phone speakers, a desktop computer, laptop, or smart TV. This studio required a professional audio engineer to be contracted every Sunday in order to achieve the highest quality of mix. For most churches trying to stream online, these resources are simply not available. And while I still firmly believe that the audio quality of North Point's online music was—and is—exceptional, there were still times when an off note by a singer or a missed chord from a musician would make me cringe.

Third, there will always be a disconnect between what is happening on stage during musical worship, and what's happening on the other side of the screen. I'm sure every worship leader imagines families standing around their computer or TV with arms raised singing along, *but is that reality?* I know many singers who try hard to create genuine, authentic worship moments for online audiences on Sunday mornings, while my family watching at home was making breakfast or playing with our dog at that point of the service.

So, what if we removed these hurdles completely?

SAMPLE CHURCH ONLINE SERVICE

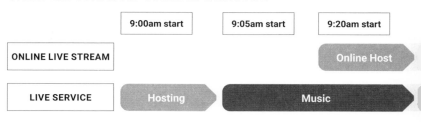

Think about it. A church that intentionally removes musical worship from their online stream could create an incentive for people who live within driving distance of the church building to show up in-person for live musical worship on Sundays.

Carey Nieuwhof wrote an article[80] recently titled: "Why attending church no longer makes sense", in which he wrote, "Increasingly, I'm convinced there's no point to merely attending. You drive all the way in to connect with three or four songs, hear the message, and then head home. All of that you could almost do by yourself in a much more convenient way. Slip on Spotify and grab the message via podcast or on demand and boom, you're covered." Carey was not calling for the closing of all church buildings. The point of his article was, "You don't attend church. You are the church." In short, there's no point in attending church if people can use podcasts and Spotify to build their own church program.

Maybe they would come back for live worship music, maybe not. But if the online stream of your church service is exactly what is happening in the room on Sundays, most will opt to stay home. After all, it's far more convenient to stay at home and watch. No need to wake everyone up early on Sunday morning, wrestle kids into the car, and navigate church parking lot traffic.

Instead of starting the online service at the same time as the in-person service, start the online service 15 to 20 minutes later as the live worship was coming to an end in the building. At that time, an online host can kick off the stream with a welcome from the lobby of the church, make any required announcements and then, as the music ends in the auditorium, they can transition seamlessly over to the speaker as they start their message. Then the service would play out as normal. ***Here's how a church online live service could look without music.***

Before I move on, it's worth noting there are people at every church who can't attend physical services because of various health issues. As an online pastor, I've shepherded many individuals and families in this sort of situation, and I would never want to deprive them of musical worship. I've spoken with many church leaders who are considering dialing back the digital once their buildings are back to capacity and I always tell them the same thing: For some people in your church community, online is their lifeline.

On the surface, a change like this would negatively impact their church experience, but there are other things we could do to fill this gap. We could post pre-recorded and pre-mixed worship content on Sundays or mid-week, or provide them with Spotify playlists to help them praise God through music.

There are alternative options if we're willing to think creatively.

And while we're thinking creatively, there are other elements we could—and I would argue *should*—add to church online services that move them beyond simply a broadcast of what happens in the room:

- **Small groups.** Making small groups available to the online community would change your online audience from being "viewers" into "participants" (more on online groups in chapter 14).
- **Geo-tagged podcasts of the message.** This gives your audience a new way to access your content, and gives you a new way to connect with people (more on podcasts in chapter 13).
- **Stream a live Q&A after the online service.** This gives people the chance to ask questions (either in a chat or via social media) and interact with the service host or the person who gave the message. When North Point included time at the end of the service for people to interact with the speaker live, we always got an incredible response and positive feedback. We often announced the post-service Q&A in the room, so people who had attended physically could also engage with the speaker from the church foyer, the parking lot, or even their car as they drove home.

A church online service that included all of these elements would look like this:

CHURCH ONLINE SERVICES FOR A
METACHURCH STRATEGY

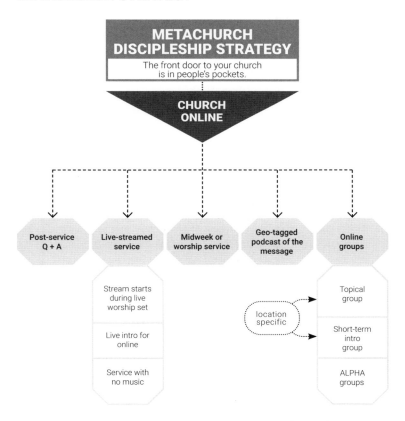

In addition to these changes to the programming of an online service, we need to change how we measure an online service.

In the first few weeks of COVID lockdowns, we all celebrated incredible statistics that showed more people were watching our online services than had ever attended our in-person services. That was until we drilled down into the data a little further. What we found was that most of our views on Facebook—anywhere from 55-85%—were for just three seconds. That's because if someone watches a video for three seconds, Facebook registers it as a view. Realistically, this means if someone who has their Facebook feed set to auto roll videos scrolls past your online live stream and pauses for a moment, they're registered as a view.

We learned that counting a view of three-seconds as an online attender of our church was the equivalent of counting the cars that drive past our church every Sunday as a physical attender.

Now to be fair, studies have shown that 65% of people who watch the first three seconds of a video, watch for at least 10 seconds, and 45% of people watching for 10 seconds continue watching for 30 seconds. But, in order to keep people who stumble onto your feed to continue watching, you would need to provide a pretty compelling incentive. This is where the other features of the MetaChurch model—like the H.O.T. intro—would come in to replace the five-minute countdown most churches use to start their live stream.

At North Point, we made the decision not to count any views that were less than five minutes. That was the benchmark we set to identify a person who had intentionally engaged with our service online. This prioritized watch time over views.

THE BLOCKBUSTER CHURCH?

And one more thing before we move on.

Many pundits have made comparisons between Blockbuster, the video store giant of the 1990s, and the brick-and-mortar church buildings, saying that church leaders who do not embrace online services are like Blockbuster, while churches that stream services are more like Netflix. For those who don't know, there was a time when Blockbuster owned more than 9000 video-rental stores in the United States, and were opening a new brick-and-mortar store every 17 hours[81]! At their peak in 1999, Blockbuster had the opportunity to purchase rival company[82], Netflix, for $50 million, but turned down the offer. It was only a few years after this that Blockbuster was being undercut by Netflix and Redbox, who were reimagining video rental in the digital age. Blockbuster eventually filed for bankruptcy in 2010[83], and at the time of writing, there is just one store left in the world in Bend, Oregon;

which, in August 2020 was listed for rental on Airbnb for $4 a night[84].

So you can probably see why the comparison is made between churches that are focussed on in-person attendance and Blockbuster.

For some people in your church community, online is their lifeline.

On the surface, this is a fair comparison. But remember, Blockbuster did not go bankrupt because they *didn't* adopt digital technology, but because they adopted it *too late*. It took Blockbuster almost five years to introduce the same services that Netflix offered and by that time, according to some reports, Netflix had already signed on 3 million subscribers.

According to a report in Business Insider[85] in 2020, Blockbuster management "were too busy making money in their video stores to imagine a time when people would no longer want or need them. And in a bid to rescue their business, their answer at the time was to fight fire with fire. At one point they even opened up rental kiosks, a little bit like a vending machine, but all of these attempts were based on either outdated technology or outdated business models, whereas Netflix at the time, did the opposite; they saw the future of video rentals and innovated for the future by offering streaming. Blockbuster didn't seem to understand how the next generation, particularly millennials who grew up in a world without hard-copy media like DVDs and CDs, would react to video-on-demand as technology improved. And that's why Netflix, Amazon Prime, YouTube, and Hulu, are still in business, while Blockbuster got left behind."

While you can find similarities between Blockbuster and the modern Church, it's not because of a focus on brick-and-mortar locations. Rather, just like Blockbuster, much of the modern Church lacks creative innovation. The Church is lagging because we're not being innovative in *using* technology. Technology is not at odds with tradition. Like James, the brother of Jesus, said:

"It is my judgment, therefore, that we should not make it difficult for the Gentiles who are turning to God"
ACTS 15:19 NIV

We need to do whatever it takes to make it easy for people to turn to God. If this means live streaming services online, let's live stream services online. If it means removing five-minute countdown from the start of the online service, shouldn't we be prepared to do it— the same with live streamed music? If sharing a first century message with 21st century methods makes it easier for people to turn to God, shouldn't we be prepared to do that?

Likewise, if your church decides that the best way for you to make it easy for people in your local community to turn to God is to choose *not* to stream Sunday services in favor of in-person community, then do that!

At the start of this chapter I quoted C.S. Lewis as saying the perfect church service is one that allows us to turn our full attention to God. That may seem obvious, but it's not a layup. Sometimes, it requires us to remove any element, no matter how long it's been a regular component of your service or how much tradition is behind it, that gets in the way of people experiencing God. Only you know what that might be for your context.

Keep reading if you're ready for some new possibilities.

CHAPTER 13

THE POWER OF PODCASTS

"

Success is just a war of attrition. Sure, there's an element of talent you should probably possess. But if you just stick around long enough, eventually something is going to happen.

DAX SHEPARD, HOST OF *THE ARMCHAIR EXPERT* PODCAST

IF THERE WAS ONE THING that defined Christianity in 2021, it was people refreshing their podcast feed to see if the latest episode of *The Rise and Fall of Mars Hill* had dropped.

The Rise and Fall of Mars Hill, produced by Christianity Today, chronicled the history of Mars Hill Church, which was started in Seattle in 1996 by self-confessed "angry prophet" preacher Mark Driscoll. The episodic podcast became required listening for anyone in Christian ministry in 2021, or for anyone even thinking about going into Christian ministry. When the first episode, titled "Who Killed Mars Hill?" was released on June 8, 2021, it was as if the Christian world finally had its version of a murder mystery podcast. This was the Jesus version of *Over My Dead Body* or *Crime Junkie*.

While I will choose to leave the critiques of the podcast's content and consequences to Christian blog writers, journalists, and my Twitter feed, there's no doubt *The Rise and Fall of Mars Hill* signaled a definitive shift in the faith podcast landscape. There had never been a narrative-style Christian podcast of this quality, which is a credit to the show's host, writer, and storyteller, Mike Cosper, who showed church leaders what was possible with this medium.

Podcasts were started in 2004, when Adam Curry, former MTV video jockey, and software developer Dave Winer, coded a program known as iPodder, to download Internet radio to their Apple iPod. What they couldn't know at the time was that they had just started an entirely new industry. According to data from Pew Research[87] and PodcastHosting.org[87], more people than ever are listening to podcasts. They found:

- 41% of Americans aged 12 or older have listened to a podcast in the past month, up from 37% in 2020 and 9% in 2008.
- 36% of Canadians listen to podcasts at least every month.
- 25% of Australians listen to podcasts at least every month.

And when it comes to Christian podcasts, Statista research[88] shows that faith podcasts make up 16% of the entire podcast market, making this genre more popular than political, self help, and pop culture podcasts.

Not only is there a growing number of podcasts in faith and Christian categories, but there are more listeners than ever before according to podcast hosting service Blubrry[89]. Their research shows that, "over the past decade, religious podcast listeners (as measured by downloads) have increased by 85% on average per year."

Up until 2021 and *The Rise and Fall of Mars Hill*, Christian podcasts typically ranged in style from church sermons and theological interviews, to devotionals and Christian self-help programs. But in a MetaChurch model, a podcast can be so much more—something in between Christianity Today's flagship content and your standard church sermon. So what if podcasts were a communication channel that churches used with a purpose instead of out of habit?

Like a lot of churches, North Point turned its Sunday message into a podcast every Monday morning. We also had a few ministries that recorded podcast episodes every other week. In 2016, we made a concerted effort to use our podcasts to connect with our audience, not just to broadcast content. To this end, we established three strategic podcast goals. They were:

1. **Establish a clear call to action for our podcast audience.**
    Podcasts needed to be geo-tagged so a person listening from Atlanta would be encouraged to visit one of our Atlanta-area churches in-person while someone listening from outside of Atlanta was encouraged to attend our online church service.

2. **Include updated content, especially around major seasonal events.**
    We wanted to be able to include seasonal information about our church (Christmas and Easter services, for example) across our back catalog of podcast episodes. Data showed that people did not always listen to our podcast episodes in order, so we wanted to be able to add and remove time-sensitive information as required. For example, we wanted to be able to promote our Easter service times in a podcast episode recorded in October three or four years earlier, then remove it after the Easter weekend.

3. **Detailed analytics.**
    We wanted to know as much information about our podcast listeners as we did about our YouTube viewers. This meant tracking where people were listening from, how long they listened to an episode, what device and app they were using to listen to our content, and what keyword searches led them to a specific podcast episode.

What if, instead of just posting the audio from Sunday's message as a podcast, you developed a podcast *on* purpose, *for* a purpose? Your church podcast can be so much more than just a one-way broadcast medium. It can be a powerfully effective tool to help you build relationships between your church and your community.

But without a clear strategy, creating a podcast is the audio equivalent of throwing spaghetti at the wall. Here are four questions to ask about your church podcast so you can develop a podcast strategy of your own.

1. **What is the goal for your podcast?**
    Whether you want people to decide to follow Jesus by the end of every podcast episode, take a deeper dive into the Bible, or just provide another option for the people in your church to engage with your message, understanding the purpose for posting a podcast is paramount (that's a lot of "p's"). A podcast is more than an

administrative task for the production or media team at the end of a Sunday. Your podcast is a chance to put Jesus and your church on display, so give it a goal and a purpose.

2. Who is your podcast for?

Is your church podcast just for the people in your church community, or do you want to reach people in the wider community where God has called you to serve? Your answer to this question may require you to create a second podcast. This is what Andy Stanley and Craig Groeschel have done with their leadership podcasts in order to reach leaders beyond the church world. If you want to reach parents, your family ministry team may decide to create their own podcast. Asking who your podcast content is for will determine a large part of your podcast strategy.

3. What next step do you want your audience to take?

A church podcast is the marketing equivalent of a sales funnel. As such, you need to let your audience know how they can connect with you and engage with your church. If they don't realize they can, they're probably not going to try. Give your audience a call to action or a next step they can take once they've listened to an episode that has particularly connected with them. This may direct them to a website, invite them to an in-person event, encourage them to read a passage of Scripture or a Bible devotional, or ask them to send an email—to list just a few. The point is, you need to let people know what you want them to do once they've engaged with your podcast.

4. How will you measure success?

The goal for your podcast must be measurable. If you want people to subscribe to an email list, how many listeners do you expect to subscribe after every episode? How many new listeners do you want at the end of every month? What would be a good listener retention rate for your podcast? It's awesome to have a goal for your church podcast, but you have to have a way of measuring if what you're doing is actually working toward your goal. Now let me add a disclaimer here. As with all church analytics, we don't measure numbers so we can post self-congratulatory tweets about how much our audience is growing. As I said before, numbers matter because people count. Every listener or viewer is a person you want to connect with so you can bring them hope and encouragement.

INNOVATING WITH PODCASTS

Turning the Sunday sermon audio into a podcast is a great start, but it's also the simplest type of podcast a church can have. What might it look like for your church to innovate with this medium?

- You could record a podcast that is an extension of Sunday's message, by interviewing the speaker or pastor about the content of their message and how listeners can apply it in the context of their family or community. This could be a quick 20 minutes of information.
- Record interviews with the local business leaders who attend your church about how their faith has positively impacted their business ventures.
- Use the podcast platform as a discipleship tool. Developing a 10-15 minute Bible study or devotional podcast published mid-week could be a huge help for your church community to take the next step in their faith journey.

This is what Mark Batterson and the team at National Community Church did in 2020. "What we've done unintentionally as churches and as pastors is foster a spiritual codependency," Batterson told me in November 2021. "What I mean by that is that people can come to church on Sunday, check a box, and then check out Monday to Friday because you got your weekly dose. When COVID-19 hit, we couldn't gather for a year and two weeks, so what we did was start NCC Daily, which is a daily podcast. Our motivation was realizing that the only ceiling on people's intimacy with God and impact on the world is daily spiritual disciplines, so let's focus on that. It's about thinking outside of the box and outside of that Sunday rhythm."

The point is to try new things. Get outside of that Sunday to Sunday rhythm. Think outside the box. Be creative. Innovate. Measure. Try again. Innovate more.

Now, you may be feeling like you've just drunk from a podcast fire hydrant. But let me counter that with some advice from Dax Shepard, the host of *Armchair Expert*, one of the most popular podcasts on the planet. He reminds us that success in the world of podcasts doesn't come overnight, "but if you just stick around long enough, eventually something is going to happen." And what we hope will happen is that the content you work so hard at creating becomes more accessible and discoverable to the very people you are trying to reach.

CHAPTER 14

CITY GROUPS, THE UPPER ZOOM, AND BIBLE APPS

"

*We have found that some unchurched people
are more open to connecting in a home
before they are willing to visit a church.*

ANDY STANLEY

WHEN I STARTED AS AN online pastor in 2008 at Liquid Church in New Jersey, one of the first things I tried to do was establish hybrid small groups.

The idea was to invite people from different locations around the world to join an in-person small group in New Jersey via video link. Back then, the only real option was Skype, so we had people from out-of-state and people in a different country Skype call into the group every week. While this was a good idea, the technology in 2008 wasn't ready to support the process. The video calls would drop in and out during the small group meeting, which meant every interaction would get cut off, and people in the room had to either restart the computer or reset the wifi to get a better connection. In the end, it was more of an irritation than a win.

Despite the frustration, I persisted with annoying the in-person small group leaders for another six months before throwing in the towel and deciding to wait until technology caught up with the idea. It did eventually catch up, and now churches have multiple options to integrate video technology into a small group strategy. In fact, technology caught up so much that one of the most well-known and longest-running small group programs in the world developed an online strategy in 2020.

At the start of 2020, more than 26,000,000[90] people had reportedly been through the Alpha Course, a 10-week in-person small group class that answers people's questions about faith. Prior to this, Nicky Gumbel, the man behind the world-famous Alpha Course, had never considered online small groups. It wasn't until the COVID pandemic forced him to move small groups to a digital environment that he made the change. In an interview he did for the Carey Nieuwhof Leadership Podcast[91], Gumbel admitted he was shocked with how well they worked. "Right from day one people were being honest, open," Gumbel said. "I don't know what it is. Whether it's less threatening because you don't think you'll necessarily see them again or what it is, but they were right from the beginning saying I'm at narcotics anonymous or I'm doing this or that. [People were] talking very openly about their personal circumstances. Therefore the relationships within the group formed so quickly. I mean, it was amazing."

Alpha Course Online also led to more than 50,000 Australians participating in the new online version in 2020. "The introduction of Alpha Online has led to the inclusion of people previously unable or unwilling to physically go to a church," Melinda Dwight, National Director of Alpha Australia, told Eternity news[92] in August 2021. "You've got people with young kids who can't go out, people who are disabled, people who find it hard to drive at night—it's just really reaching a different audience online, which has been amazing."

This is a good example of a ministry innovating during a crisis.

Mark Sayers, author and lead pastor at Red Church in Melbourne, says a crisis like COVID can be an opportunity for the Church to move forward[93]. "When a crisis happens most of us can feel tempted to go back to what we know. [But] what if everything that we've been living in our leadership journeys up to this moment has actually been preparing people for this moment? What if this is now the moment where God wants to do something? He's disrupted, he's got the world's attention, he's frozen people in place, and we have this incredible technological ability that the apostle Paul would have killed for, to project our message to the world, to show Jesus' love, to lead and speak vision."

ONLINE GROUPS 2.0

So, with all this in mind, how do we leverage technology to help people connect and stay engaged in small groups? Glad you asked.

Here are four options you can use in conjunction with in-person groups.

City Groups

City Groups (outlined in chapter 6) are a way to connect people who watch your online services from a specific town or city with others who are also watching from the same location. When we started trialing this at North Point in 2017, we had hundreds of people from across North America requesting to start, join, lead, or host a City Group.

Here's a process that can work for you:

1. Someone signs up. This might seem obvious, but you can't have a group if no one signs up.
2. Connect with them and confirm their location and level of interest in a group.
3. If they are interested in leading a City Group, provide some small group leadership coaching, help identify and connect other online viewers in their area, and then do regular check-ins with the group leaders.
4. If they are interested in joining a City Group, make an introduction with a leader in their town.
5. If they are the first in the area to show interest, vision cast for why they might be a good fit to lead a group themselves.

That's it.

Of course, you have some administrative details to track: names, addresses, contact numbers, and group members. But the administrative work is the same as you would do for any small group at your church.

Zoom Groups

A month into the COVID-19 lockdowns, I learned someone had purchased the URL zoom.church. My first reaction was "brilliant." My next reaction was frustration that I hadn't thought of buying the URL (I have an issue with purchasing URLs; which I'll eventually deal with in a different book).

The URL was purchased by Influencers Church, a multinational church that started in South Australia so they could start Zoom small groups to complement their live-streamed services on YouTube. On the splash page[94] that zoom.church links to, the church announced that the purpose of a Zoom group is to help people "stay connected as we digitally gather online for worship, an encouraging message and communion every weekend."

Mark Batterson's National Community Church in Washington, D.C. also opted to use Zoom for small groups, creating "The Upper Zoom," a place for the church to gather together for prayer. In fact, the church developed a daily prayer routine on the platform at 7:14AM each day, to "pray for racial reconciliation, for healings, for peace, for revival—in other words, for God's kingdom to come and His will to be done!" Batterson explained.

All this to say, Zoom has become a viable platform for small groups, whether they are all-digital, or a hybrid of online and in-person. But a successful Zoom group doesn't just happen.

Here are a few tips for someone leading a small group on Zoom:

- **Have everything ready in advance.** Trying to manage your Bible study notes while managing the Zoom controls can get confusing if you're not prepared.
- **Announce the plan.** Up front, let everyone know the agenda— what you plan to cover and how long you plan for each part of the meeting. You can also post this in the chat window for the visual learners in the room.
- **Start with fun.** Plan something fun to kick off every meeting, and get people in the mood. This may involve texting the group before the meeting and asking them to have their favorite

meme ready, or to set up a virtual background, or to bring their own snacks and drinks, etc.
- **Finish early.** Since more people than ever are using Zoom for work meetings, Zoom fatigue is a real thing. That's why I suggest planning for shorter group meetings than you would if you were in a physical space.

Facebook Groups and Rooms

Facebook Groups provide another way for church leaders to establish small groups. An existing small group can set up a private group for members to engage with each other outside of group times, or specifically during group meetings.

Facebook also launched Rooms during COVID, to allow people to connect via video chat. As Nona Jones, head of faith-based partnership at Facebook writes in her book, *From Social Media To Social Ministry: A Guide To Digital Discipleship*, "It [Facebook Rooms] is a powerful way to keep small groups working together during the week and is an important ministry tool for churches desiring to create spaces within Facebook for members to connect and grow."

Facebook Rooms can be used instead of Zoom, which means there is no need for people to become familiar with a new platform, if they're not using Zoom already. Using Facebook for video calls also eliminates any Zoom fatigue people may feel after a week of working remotely.

YouVersion Bible Studies

The YouVersion Bible app is another option for churches to use for small groups and discipleship. The app's broad popularity makes it an accessible option for creative pastors to use as part of a small group study. Pastors from around the world, myself included, have become part of the teaching partner team at YouVersion, writing and publishing reading plans within the app that incorporate Bible readings and devotional content. On top of this, at the start of 2020, YouVersion introduced Verse of the Day Stories, with well-known pastors and ministry leaders providing two-minute devotional videos based on the—you guessed it—verse of the day.

When church small groups follow each other on YouVersion, they can read Scripture together, send each other messages to discuss what they're reading, keep each other accountable through the app, and even share what they're reading on social media. And at the time of writing, YouVersion is beta testing new features that will allow churches to:

- create organization profiles
- share content and notifications directly with their church community groups
- access enhanced data about their church community
- stream online services directly in the app

These updates will allow churches to further leverage YouVersion as a small group and discipleship tool.

WhatsApp

As of July 2021, WhatsApp was the third most popular social network platform in the world behind Youtube and Facebook, with approximately two billion monthly active users. Like Facebook Rooms, WhatsApp allows group video calls, which means it can be used as an alternative to Zoom. And as a purpose-built messaging app, it can be an efficient tool for leaders to stay connected to their group.

WhatsApp also gives churches and ministries the ability to broadcast audio messages to individuals or groups. This could be a live recording of a Bible devotion or pre-recorded audio from a sermon. This content can then be discussed in group video calls or messages.

MAKING GROUPS ACCESSIBLE

Now, these digital small group ideas will not fix a small group problem at your church. If your church is already invested in a small group strategy, these ideas can help. But as my mate, Jay Kranda, online pastor at Saddleback Church in California, says, "Online doesn't fix your church but amplifies your local strengths and problems by removing all friction." If your church already has a strong small group system and strategy, then integrating technology will only make a strong foundation stronger.

When leveraged well, technology can help make small groups more accessible to more people.

Now, before we move on, let me state clearly that online video conferencing cannot and should not replace meeting people face-to-face. That's not what I'm advocating. But, as I've said before, online tools may not be our first choice but sometimes they're our only choice.

For more than 13 years, my family and I lived in the United States, away from our family and friends in Australia. For us, Zoom, FaceTime, and Skype were our only options to stay connected with the people we loved. In 2019, when our eldest daughter went on a seven-month mission trip to Guatemala, Ethiopia, and Thailand, video chat gave us the only opportunity we had to see her face and for her to see ours (although I often had to hide my face from the screen so she couldn't see me crying from missing her).

New technology can create new opportunities to enhance relationships when we give the *person* more attention than the *platform*.

The point is, new technology can create new opportunities to enhance relationships when we give the *person* more attention than the *platform*. When we do that, we begin to see how technology doesn't have to be an impediment, but a contributor—in the best way possible—to healthy small group ministries.

CHAPTER 15
REACHING THE WORLD

"

The trouble with quotes on the Internet is that it's difficult to determine whether or not they are genuine.

ABRAHAM LINCOLN

IF YOU HAD TOLD THE 12-year-old version of me that one day I would be in ministry helping church leaders through a monumental moment in Church history, I would have laughed at you.

See, I grew up in an unchurched home in the western suburbs of Melbourne, Australia, and all I wanted to be as a kid was a sports journalist.

Before I had finished my first year in college, I was working as a sports reporter for a local newspaper. By the end of my first year out of college, I was working for a sports magazine, and by the time I was 28, I was the editor of one of the oldest and highest selling sports magazines in Australia. A year later, I was working as a TV sports reporter and producer for one of the three largest television networks in Australia.

I spent the next seven years in my dream job, covering the Australian Open, English Premier League, Australian Rules football, and even interviewing celebrities such as Dwayne "The Rock" Johnson, Chris Evans, and Nicole Kidman. Then, in 2007, just after being recommended for a position at ESPN's flagship program—SportsCenter—my wife Meg and I felt the undeniable call into ministry.

Ugh.

And so, in 2008, I left my job as a TV sports reporter and producer to become the 8th online pastor in the world at a church in Morristown, New Jersey.

I share this because up until that call into ministry, I had never really shared my faith. By the time I started following Jesus, I was so focussed on my career, that sharing my faith with others was never really a priority. After I got married, my family and I were part of a local church where I was on the leadership team, oversaw the music team, and preached a handful of times a year, but I never thought about sharing my faith personally. I was so busy in my day-to-day world of work and family that I guess I thought being involved with our church was enough. That didn't change until I got into ministry—when I really started taking seriously the importance of people sharing their faith in the real world.

If it hasn't been clear to this point, let me spell out that most of the ideas in this book work as evangelism tools—from short YouTube content to shareable social media posts and podcasts. That's because in a MetaChurch model, all digital and physical channels are tools for reaching new people, and for growing your current church community.

And according to recent research, people at your church are willing to share their faith and invite people to your services. According to Barna Research[95] from December 2020, nearly two-thirds of Christians (64%) say they're open to inviting someone to attend an in-person church service, and four in 10 (40%) say they're open to inviting someone to join them for an online church service. People want to invite their family and friends to church, and it's our role as church leaders to make it as easy as possible for them to do it. One of the easiest ways is through digital evangelism opportunities.

We need to remember that sometimes the easiest way to spread the Good News is to allow people to share the Good News digitally. But it's also important to remember that, according to *Forbes*[96], people are exposed to anywhere between 4000 and 10,000 digital ads every single day. That means, if your church is going to create content people actually want to share on their own social media channels, then it has to stand out from the noise by being engaging and speaking directly to the context of your local community.

This is another reason why everything a church posts on social media, websites, podcast platforms, or YouTube needs to have a purpose and intentionality.

At North Point, everything we did as a church—whether it was our Sunday services, special events, webinars, or evangelism tools—was built on what Andy and the leadership team referred to as The Five Faith Catalysts. You can read more about them in Andy's 2012 book, *Deep and Wide: Creating Churches Unchurched People Love to Attend,* but simply, the Five Faith Catalysts are:

- Practical Teaching
- Private Disciplines
- Personal Ministry
- Providential Relationships
- Pivotal Circumstances

When it comes to sharing faith online, I believe each of these catalysts can occur in digital environments. For example:

- **Practical Teaching:** Teaching can be accessed through many online and digital channels such as YouTube, Facebook, and podcasts—not just physical attendance.
- **Private Disciplines:** Online Bibles and apps like YouVersion can play a significant role in the daily disciplines that grow a person's faith.
- **Personal Ministry:** Personal ministry opportunities do exist online if we're creative in helping people find them. Similarly, if people are encouraged to lead digital small groups, host viewing parties of services, or connect with people in online chats during an online service (for example) then this can become their own personal ministry.
- **Providential Relationships:** Social media and online video technology make providential relationships broader and more effective than ever before. Personal mentoring can happen online, and people can share their stories on any number of social media platforms.
- **Pivotal Circumstances:** A generation growing up online is experiencing more defining moments in digital spaces than ever before. The Church needs to be in these spaces helping

provide direction, insight, and hope when those pivotal circumstances arise.

Part of any discipleship process—whether online or in person—is helping people be able to share their faith in a way that's congruent with their lifestyle.

For example, if you want to connect with youth culture, try using the instant messaging app Discord, or Twitch, a live streaming platform that gets more than 140 million unique visitors every month[97]. Want to connect with kids? YouTube Kids would be a great option!

Your church can help people share their faith in digital environments by equipping them with resources, skills, and content. This can happen in many different forms on many different platforms, but the important thing is that it happens.

The MetaChurch discipleship strategy is designed to ensure that everything a church posts online, on any channel and platform, and in any format, will connect with people and help them learn about Jesus and experience his love. From Sunday services to mid-week content, social media to blog posts, the Instagram grid to online classes, the idea of everything working together to both preach the gospel to every creature (Mark 16:15) and make disciples (Matthew 28:18) is the end goal.

If you're keeping track, the following chapters connect together to offer a cohesive MetaChurch strategy:

- Chapter 7 outlines a mid-week content strategy for your church.
- Chapter 9 includes a content distribution plan.
- Chapter 10 offers a church social media strategy.
- Chapter 12 presents a church online service strategy.

The four diagrams (on the following pages) fit together to form a complete strategy.

This is just one version of the strategy. Your church may discover a different path based on the ideas above. Whatever you choose to do, work to ensure that every aspect of what you do online is linked. What your church does digitally should integrate seamlessly with what your church does physically.

After more than a decade in online ministry, I believe this represents the best version of MetaChurch using current technology, and is how the future Church will go into all the world and share the Good News.

I know that for most of you reading this book, this seems like a mission impossible, right? Yes, you want to reach more people in your local community, and you may even agree that online is a good way to do that. But this feels like

> **What your church does digitally should integrate seamlessly with what your church does physically.**

something only the North Points, Hillsongs, Elevations, Church of the Highlands, and Life Churches of the world can do. You simply don't have the time, people, or financial resources to pull something like this off. Well, before closing this chapter, let me share a simple idea with you.

For the first time in human history, we have the ability to go around the world in a moment. You could record a short video tonight on your phone, post it to YouTube, Instagram, Twitter, or any other platform, and have it go viral by the morning and be seen by millions of people. It doesn't take a lot of expensive gear or a production team. This reality gives all-new meaning to Jesus' command in Mark 16:15 to "Go into all the world and preach the gospel to all creation." We have a responsibility as church leaders to leverage this technology in any way we are able.

So no matter what size your church, your staff, or your budget, you have the same access to online platforms as anyone else, and you probably already have a $1000 camera in your pocket right now. You don't have to do everything—but you can do something.

Are you prepared to use this technology to do whatever it takes to reach the people living in the place God has called you to serve?

METACHURCH DISCIPLESHIP STRATEGY

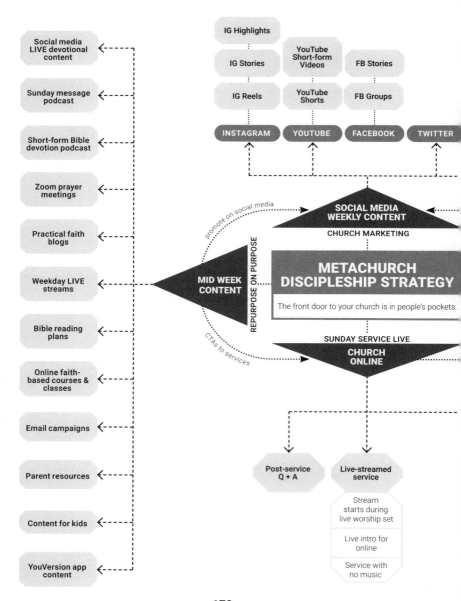

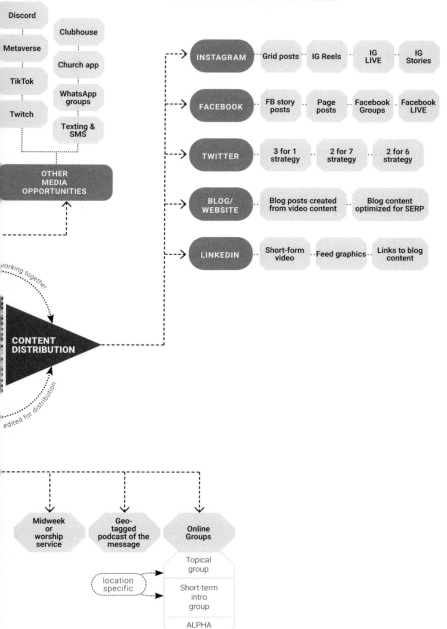

CHAPTER 16

EXPECTING THE WORST IN THE DIGITAL WORLD

"

The secret to crisis management is not good vs bad. It's preventing the bad from getting worse.

ANDY GILMAN

THERE ARE A MILLION WAYS to fail on social media—many of them self-inflicted.

From the communications director fired while on an international flight due to a pre-boarding tweet, to the BBC reporter joking in a post that the Queen had died, social media fails can have a lasting impact.

And the Church is not immune.

We have been known to create our own social media emergencies, although the definition of a social media "crisis" in the Church world may vary wildly.

It could range from the misspelling of a Hebrew word in an Instagram post (yep, I'm guilty of this), a church message receiving some negative reviews on Facebook, a speaker accidentally cursing during a live stream, pastors tweeting out their home addresses, pastors liking posts they didn't fully read, to looking insensitive during a national tragedy through scheduled tweets.

There are a lot of ways for a church to create a crisis online. And as churches continue to have a more obvious digital presence in this new technological landscape, the opportunities for missteps are greater than ever.

That's why every church should have a plan in place to prevent a bad communication situation on the Internet from getting worse. While it's true that very few churches will ever have to face national news-worthy scrutiny, there are several things that can generate negative feedback for any size church on social media. These include:

1. **A reaction to a controversial message or quote**
   People may have a negative reaction to a message quote that has been posted on one of your church social media channels—whether that quote was taken out of context or not.

2. **A theological debate gone ugly**
   A comment thread on one of your channels turns negative due to a theological disagreement.

3. **Negative publicity of a church service or event**
   Someone posts or streams a negative review of a church service or event, class, or webinar.

4. **An attack on worship leaders, hosts, or volunteers**
   The conduct of someone on staff or a volunteer during a service receives negative backlash.

5. **A reaction to staff member misconduct**
   A staff member's social media generates a negative reaction online. (To be clear, I'm talking about a personal opinion or photo a staff member posts online—not harmful behavior that requires a disciplinary protocol for a volunteer or staff member).

So how does a church staff prevent a bad situation from getting worse? The first step is to define when a crisis management plan should be implemented, and when online negativity should simply be observed or ignored. Here are the negative feedback thresholds that should determine the next steps of action:

1. **Less than five negative mentions per hour**
    Continue monitoring online activity. Compile a list of the comments for review.

2. **More than five negative mentions per hour**
    Contact other leaders in your church to review the status of the situation and begin developing a response plan.

3. **More than 15 negative mentions per hour**
    Officially roll out a social media management plan with your church social media director.

No church wants to find themselves in the middle of an online storm, but we need to be prepared for it. When a crisis arises, here's what I recommend your church's online pastor, communications director, or social media team leader should do:

1. **Determine if it's an actual crisis**
    There's a difference between a negative comment and an actual social media crisis. Would one negative comment from a weekend attender constitute a crisis? No. But sometimes when one comment is posted to social media, we go into full-blown panic mode.

2. **Track comments, posts, and tweets**
    Every church will attract negative comments and feedback regularly, so you need to monitor activity on all platforms and channels. Monitoring negative feedback should be the responsibility of the online pastor, communications director, or social media team lead. Any negative comments and posts need to be tracked across multiple platforms including: Facebook, Instagram, YouTube, Twitter, TikTok, etc.

3. **Document aggressively negative feedback**
    Aggressively negative comments are those that use profanity, include personal attacks on staff members, volunteers and other social media followers, or a persistent level of posting over a short period of time.

4. **Pause all scheduled social media posts**
    You may want to hit pause on third party scheduling apps, because you don't want to post content for engagement during a crisis.

5. Communicate with a predetermined team

If a social media crisis escalates, you need to have a list of people on staff or in the church who need to be informed to help with the situation.

6. Hide or delete posts

Deleting or hiding negative posts and comments seems like an easy solution, but it's not that simple. We need to remember that people have the right to have and share their own opinions. Freedom of speech needs to be taken into consideration. With this in mind, when it comes to hiding and deleting posts and comments provided by other people, here are three options:

- **HIDE** — Spam, posts with external websites, persistent negative accusations, and incoherent comments.
- **DELETE** — Persistent spam, profanity or foul language, explicit content, bullying other users, personal attacks, and obscene photos.
- **KEEP** — Negative comments about an event, negative feedback on an event or service, disagreements about theology. Keep these comments active, because it could make matters worse if you stop people from expressing their opinions, even when you don't agree with them.

You can also create a form that staff and key volunteers could use to report any issues on social media or fake accounts.

Finally, secure all of your accounts by changing passwords a couple of times a year, and using a password management tool such as 1Password or LastPass. I know more than a few friends in ministry who have had their social media accounts hacked, and then received an email from the people responsible asking for money to release the account.

Seriously.

Here's a DM a friend of mine received from a hacker who broke into their TikTok account in October 2021.

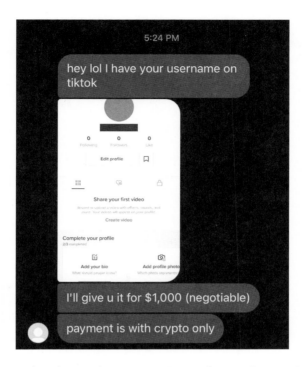

For larger churches and ministries, it may be worth investing in a "social listening" program to help you spot any potential issues on social media before they turn into a crisis. Social listening services and programs monitor and review your social media platforms for mentions and conversations related to your church or brand. These mentions can then be analyzed to discover any issues that need to be addressed, or in the positive, the results can be used to discover potential opportunities.

The point here is that, in the words of Sir Winston Leonard Spencer Churchill, Prime Minister of the United Kingdom during the Second World War, "He who fails to plan is planning to fail." And since this is a book for church leaders, I'll add a few Bible verses to close out the chapter and make it official.

*Be on your guard; stand firm in the
faith; be courageous; be strong*
1 CORINTHIANS 16:13

*Be on guard! Be alert! You do not know
when that time will come*
MARK 13:33

*So then, let us not be like others, who are
asleep, but let us be awake and sober*
1 THESSALONIANS 5:6

*Be dressed ready for service
and keep your lamps burning*
LUKE 12:35

Yeah, I know none of these specifically speak to the context of social media crisis, but my point is that whatever you decide to do, as always, do it with intentionality. And do it ahead of time, before there is a crisis, so you're not caught off guard when a crisis eventually comes knocking. C.S. Lewis once wrote, "what a man does when he is taken off his guard is the best evidence for what sort of man he is."

Don't let the evidence show you were unprepared.

PLANNING
AHEAD

CHAPTER 17
THE FUTURE CHURCH?

"

Today's heresy is tomorrow's orthodoxy.

ERWIN MCMANUS

COULD YOU IMAGINE IF, AT the start of 2020, you had bought stock in Zoom?

In January 2020, shares for the video conferencing platform were trading for just over $76 a share in the U.S. Nine months later, Zoom shares were going for $559 each—that's a 635% increase! If any of us saw that coming and bought Zoom stocks, we'd probably be panning for retirement right now!

I mean, wouldn't it be awesome if you could predict the future like that!?

But, even after all this time in online church, I'm reluctant to predict what the future might hold. Part of the reason for my reluctance is because of the backlash I received the last time I tried to predict the future of the Church.

In March 2019, I got a call from an editor at FOXNews.com asking if I would be interested in writing an op-ed on the future of the Church and the role live streaming, Youtube, and church online needed to play. They essentially wanted me to predict the future of the Church . . . so I did. After handing the piece in, Fox News ran it under the headline: Church as we know it is over. Here's what's next[98].

The article was met with almost immediate opposition. There was so much opposition in fact, that within minutes of the op-ed going live, it was featured on the front page of foxnews.com, right next to a story about Donald Trump and Nancy Pelosi . . . and a story about Alyssa Milano's identity crisis. It must have been a slow news day because a little online pastor from Australia should not get placed right next to Alyssa Milano!

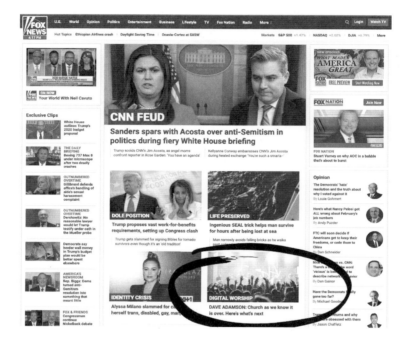

By the end of the week, more than 5000 people had commented on the story. What I thought was an insightful and well-researched report based on data, research, and actual ministry experience, was condemned, with all but five of the comments being *against* my predictions!

Two of the comments that stood out the most to me were the one that suggested I looked like "a spaced out drug addict" (fair call, I suppose) and the one that said my prediction about the Church's future would take away people's will to live! My favorite part of this last one was that it was provided by someone who went by the name "Hope faith love."

Let's be honest for a second. The Church has never been great at predicting the future, much less changing course once we realize the future has arrived and looks nothing like we'd hoped. Rather than trying to predict a future, the goal should be having a plan to respond to the future—whatever that looks like.

One of my favorite theologians, Abraham Joshua Heschel, once said, "We are closer to God when we are asking questions than when we think we have the answers." In short, when we stop being curious, we stop growing. As church leaders, when we stop asking questions about our model, our traditions, or our church environments, we stop being innovative. This is why a lot of church leaders were asking the wrong question during the COVID pandemic. Instead of asking, "God, *when* can we get out of this crisis?"; we should have been asking, "God, *what* can we get out of this crisis?"

As the Church approaches new technological advances in the future, it's important for us to remain curious and ask questions. As church leaders we need to give ourselves and our teams permission to dream when it comes to sharing the life-changing message of Jesus with the world.

"It's far more limiting to try and predict what might happen[99]," says Bobby Gruenewald, pastor and innovation leader at Life.Church, and the founder of the YouVersion Bible app. "I try to focus more on speed and agility so that we can respond quickly and are geared toward learning." I agree! *This* is the future of the Church: Pastors and leaders who are committed to learning and growing, open to new ideas, and willing to innovate and ask questions—not just assume they already have the answers. And isn't this the way of Jesus? In the Gospels we see that Jesus asked 307 questions, so maybe it's time we learned to ask a few of our own.

Church as we know it is over. Here's what's next.

Here are some questions to consider when it comes to your church model:

- What questions are you currently asking about your model for doing church?
- What questions are you allowing your staff to ask?
- Are you prepared to get answers to questions that may scare you?
- What questions *should* you be asking about your church model?
- Are your questions too small when it comes to your church method? If so, why do you think that is?
- How can your church reimagine what is possible?
- Do you deliberately hesitate to change your model? Why?
- Does your church have an aversion to technology, or is there something more that's stopping you from innovating?
- What would it take for your church to become more creative in its model?
- Are you open to the idea of regularly asking questions about your church model? If not, why?

If we want to understand where we need to go, we first have to understand where we are.

Much of our faith practices have been handed down through traditions. It doesn't mean they're wrong or bad or aren't useful, but often traditions dictate how we do things. It could be that it's time to see traditions for what they are. Like my friend, Stuart Hall, Director of Student Leadership for Orange, says, "Traditions are simply peer pressure from dead people and outdated social constructs."

So, what if instead of letting traditions define us as we move into the future, we were able to set certain traditions aside and lean into new ideas that will propel the Church forward to reach more people? I've never met a pastor who didn't want to reach unchurched people, and leveraging online technology is the best way to do just that.

If we want all the benefits of Acts 2:47, where God "added to their number daily those who were being saved," we need to put in the work of Acts 2:46 where it says, "Every day they continued to meet together in the temple courts. They broke bread in their homes and ate together with glad and sincere hearts." To do this, we have to accept that it's time to think beyond our organized weekly meetings.

Keeping up with those Acts 2:46 daily meetings in the postmodern world require us to creatively use technology that we may not have considered before.

As church leaders, when we stop asking questions about our model, our traditions, or our church environments, we stop being innovative.

TEXTING

Take texting and SMS marketing for example. According to research conducted[100] in 2021, 3.8 billion people in the world own smart-phones, and the open rate for an SMS is 98%, making it an incredible tool for engagement. Using services like Text In Church, Community App, or SuperPhone to follow up with guests and engage with members are perfect opportunities just waiting to be taken advantage of.

VIRTUAL REALITY

When Mark Zuckerberg announced Facebook's rebrand to "Meta" in October 2021 and declared his company would be all-in on virtual reality, many of us wondered what this would mean for the Church. I'm sure church leaders around the world were asking how Zuckerberg's "metaverse" would change the way we do church—and is "metaverse" different from Marvel's multi-verse? But while Facebook, sorry, *Meta*, thrust VR into the spotlight, it's actually been around for years. My friend, Metaverse Pastor (yes, that's his official title) DJ Soto, the Bishop of Virtual Reality Church (again, his real title), told me recently that he believes the Church will shift virtual in the not too distant future.

"The next generation of church will shift from a physical experience as the primary and 'approved' way to experience church, to virtual and augmented reality experiences," DJ told me. "This doesn't mean physical gatherings will go away. It only means that the physical gathering will be a lateral or equal experience to mixed reality expressions. Whether they realize it or not, churches are now metaverse churches that may or may not have a physical location. Churches who embrace this mindset will thrive, and those who don't will struggle."

I first met DJ when I was his online pastor at Liquid Church in New Jersey in 2008. The first time I met him in-person however was 10 years later at Facebook HQ, two years after he had started preaching in virtual reality worlds.

"We've had great success in creating church communities inside the metaverse." DJ explains. "We've planted four metaverse churches with more on the way. Each church is led by different leaders with a volunteer team to help with all aspects of the church. I believe our greatest success has been to discover and experience that we can replicate all the functions of the church in the metaverse."

Now, I'm not asking you to start a virtual reality church—yet (although according to app tracking company Annie App[101], the Oculus VR app was the most downloaded app in the U.S. on Christmas Day, 2021). All I'm asking is for you to ask questions about your current church model.

"I believe one of the key things is to start handing over the leadership decisions to younger thinkers who can easily navigate the coming technological revolution," DJ encourages. "Let the younger generation decide the ecclesiological route to navigate. Empower them to move forward." DJ suggests every pastor should create space for the young leaders in their church to dream and plan what the future of the church might be—and to create opportunities to experiment.

ARTIFICIAL INTELLIGENCE

What about AI? Will the future of the Church be found in machine learning? Artificial intelligence is one of those areas that even people in the digital church space are reluctant to bring up in polite company when discussing the future of the Church. I used to think this was because too many current church leaders grew up in the 80's and 90's watching *Terminator* movies, and so the thought of Arnold Schwarzenegger leading Skynet Church with a choir of Cyberdyne Systems Model 101 Series 800 Terminators kept us awake at night (although every pastor in the world would love to hear their parishioners say "I'll be back"). Turns out we just don't fully understand AI and machine learning—even though it's already something most of us use regularly—and the modern Church has developed a hard-earned reputation for shunning things it doesn't understand.

It didn't help that in a 2017 report in *The Atlantic*[102], U.S.-based religion writer, Jonathan Merritt, described AI as "the greatest threat to Christian theology since Charles Darwin's *On the Origin of Species*." Or that vox.com ran an article in January 2020 titled, "Robot priests can bless you, advise you, and even perform your funeral",[103] about Mindar the robot preaching a message at a 400-year-old Buddhist temple in Kyoto, Japan. But real world applications of AI and machine learning already exist. If you have ever told Siri to, "Play the latest Lauren Daigle album," or asked Alexa, "What was the robot in *Terminator* called?" then you've used AI. Siri and Alexa operate by artificial intelligence, and no one is expecting our Google assistant to suddenly turn deadly (which may be exactly what they want us to think . . . cue *Terminator* music . . . da da dun da dun).

But I agree with Bobby Gruenewald who, in an AP News report[104] in 2018 about YouVersion introducing AI into its popular Bible app said, "As technologies emerge and create new possibilities, it's important to us that the Bible be at the forefront of innovation."

MOVING FORWARD

The future of the church will not necessarily belong to leaders who jump on every new platform, channel, and app that comes along, but to those leaders who see technology through the lens of innovation and opportunity.

In 1739, the famous methodist preacher George Whitefield started preaching outdoors to miners and other unchurched people in the English port town of Bristol. Whitefield saw an opportunity to reach people, and took it. His contemporary, John Wesley, was initially against the radical innovation of open-air preaching, considering it "vile" and "strange"[105]. He didn't see the opportunity to reach people through outdoor preaching, preferring the "decency and order"[106] of a church building. "I could scarce reconcile myself at first to this strange way of preaching in the fields, having been all my life so tenacious of every point relating to decency and order that I should have thought the saving of souls almost a sin if it had not been done in a church," Wesley wrote in his journal in 1739. But after seeing Whitefield in action and asking questions about his preferences, Wesley started preaching with Whitefield in Bristol, and the Wesleyan Revival followed.

Wesley saw the benefit of a new opportunity and innovated his personal preference to take advantage of it.

Remember that 2021 research project by Springtide I mentioned in chapter 10? That was the one that surveyed 2500 members of Generation Z and revealed that nine out of 10 young people didn't hear from a faith leader during the pandemic. How we respond to a report like that reveals a lot about how we're wired for ministry because we all read stats, numbers, data, or analytics with a bias. I've shared that research with a lot of ministry people and received polarizing responses. Some have reacted with a bias toward making sure their church is doing everything possible to connect with young people, others have cautiously wanted to dig into the research more, some have brushed off the research because it wasn't relevant to their context, and still others reflected about how they stand on the positive side of the equation. And then there have been many who—because of their own personal story, ministry experience, or the story of someone they are close to—have been moved emotionally and wanted to connect with every single teenager on the negative side of this research.

It's the same when it comes to church online, digital ministry, and this book.

Some people will nerd out on the technical side of online ministry, and others will want to make sure their church is doing everything possible to leverage technology to reach and connect with their community. Some will maintain that Hebrews 10:25 is clear about meeting together physically so they won't consider increasing their online presence, others will want to update their church's YouTube thumbnails in order to improve their click-through-rate, and some will continue with business as usual.

Helping your church thrive in the future is not about being the first on new platforms, updating your website, or simply posting more content online. The church leaders who will be well-placed for the future are those who are open to innovation, testing new opportunities and listening to experts.

That's where we're headed next.

CHAPTER 18

SO ... WHAT'S NEXT?

"

In the future Church, leaders who are willing to change their methods will amplify their mission. Leaders who don't, won't.

CAREY NIEUWHOF

AS WE CLOSE OUR TIME together, I want us to do more than just imagine how to make the most of the cultural moment we are currently in. I want us to dream about what is possible beyond today.

The churches that will be future-proof are not those that jump onto the latest technology, app, or social media trend, but those that can continue to ask questions about their model and method, and remain curious about technology. As a dad, one of the words of advice I've reiterated to my three daughters throughout their life is an uncredited quote that says, "A smart person will give smart answers, but a wise person will ask smart questions." Every morning before putting them on the school bus I would give them the shorthand version of this quote, encouraging them to "ask smart questions today." This is my advice for the Church too. We need to be asking smart questions about technology, smart questions about our model for doing church, smart questions about how we're connecting with the local community we're serving, and smart questions about how we're engaging with our church family and helping them take the next step in their faith journey.

We need to ask questions like:

- How can I use keyword phrases to reach more people?
- How can Facebook Groups improve connections at my church?
- What can I learn about preaching from YouTubers?
- How can I give purpose to my church's Instagram posts?
- Why are students messaging each other through social media DMs?
- Why was TikTok the most downloaded app in the world[107] on Christmas Day, 2021?

And we also need to ask smart questions about how we personally use technology. Consider how much you rely on technology and ask smart questions about how often you're taking breaks from being online. That's right, breaks from technology!

Social media and the Internet should enhance your life, not become your life.

If church leaders can get behind asking smart questions about technology, the Church won't be left behind by technology. Asking smart questions will keep us open-handed, innovative, and ready for the future.

I remember my friend Reggie Joiner once saying from the stage at Orange Conference in Atlanta that, "Everything changes when it's someone you know." That statement has had a profound impact on me, and I've probably quoted it once a week ever since. No matter what the issue or the polarizing argument, everything changes when someone you know and love is impacted. My three daughters, Chelsea, Ella, and Jordyn, have grown up in an online world, which influences why I want to encourage church leaders to integrate digital technology. I want my daughters' church to stay connected to my girls, and encourage them throughout the week—not just on Sundays. I also have unchurched family who I love and want to see connected to Jesus, so I want the churches near them to post optimized content on YouTube that answers the life questions they're asking.

> "A smart person will give smart answers, but a wise person will ask smart questions."

Reggie is right; everything *does* change when it's someone you know. So who are the people you know who would be positively impacted if they could connect with a church digitally, and then become part of a physical community?

Regardless of what technology the future holds, the one prediction I will happily make is that there is a day coming when church leaders won't feel the need to denigrate online church in order to raise up on-site church.

In the same way that Peter and James led the early church at the Council of Jerusalem, two decades after Jesus' resurrection, to a com-

> **Social media and the Internet should enhance your life, not become your life.**

promise between the Jewish and Gentile believers, I believe a similar compromise will exist in the Church between physical space and cyberspace. When this happens the church will once again *"not make it difficult"* for anyone who is turning to God (Acts 15:19).

And shouldn't that be our goal—to make it as easy as possible for people to hear the Gospel and become disciples?

Realistically, I know that all the stats, research, reports, and motivational quotes from leaders on the cutting edge may not be enough to convince you to begin rethinking your church's discipleship model or impact how you engage technology. And maybe that's a good thing. Maybe none of these things should be what compels you to rethink the way church exists in an online world. Maybe all you need to do is think of the next generation. This is what convinces me to keep asking questions. It's why I keep my daughters at the forefront of my mind when I imagine what the next iteration of church could look like. Because, at the end of the day, this is about so much more than method or model, about technology or platforms. This is about the people we love coming up behind us and the Church we want them to inherit.

That's why I dedicated this book to my girls. I want them to inherit a church that is better positioned to deal with the future. And my guess is, when you think about the people you love coming up behind you, you will feel the same urgency that I do. Are we willing to try something new for them? For the next generation and the generations behind them? For the sake of the gospel?

To close, I want to leave you with some thoughts from some of the most thoughtful and innovative church leaders I know, as they share what they see is next for the Church. Imagining a MetaChurch may seem scary, but the best news is, we aren't alone! There's a whole community of people who are willing to take the message of the Gospel into this brave new world. And my hope is, you will be a part of it.

So what's next for the Church? I'll let my friends take it from here.

MARK BATTERSON
Lead Pastor at National Community Church

"I could give the standard answer and say the future of the Church is going to be more hybrid, but it's going to be different for every church. Oswald Chambers said, 'Let God be as original with others as he was with you', so I think we need to realize that how the future looks will depend on your church and whether you're an urban church or a rural church for example. So, the one thing I keep coming back to is a quote from, R.T. Kendall who said, 'Sometimes the greatest opposition to what God wants to do next, comes from those who were on the cutting edge of what God did last.' That quote keeps me on my knees when I think about the future. That keeps me humble."

KENNY JAHNG
Chief Innovation Officer for Big Click Syndicate

"The general, critical, mistake in leadership culture found in many churches today is that the pastors and leaders reinforce the ostrich mentality surrounding gaps in competence. They ignore it, downplay it, and obviously underestimate the importance of it. And I believe much of it stems from fear—fear of losing authority and power and influence. Growth oriented leaders, especially in the marketplace, embrace a culture of skills acquisition and development, and so they pay for outside consultants to come in to inform and teach in areas that the internal team isn't fully versed with. They hire freelancers, part-time and full-time, to bring in new specialization and competence for the organization, but not enough churches and ministries do this.

"I believe a lot of this comes from the unintended consequences of the patron financial model of churches. Without having the need to pay attention to market feedback, survival and longevity of a ministry relies on satisfying those that give to the church—who may or may not under-stand just how large of a gap the church currently has with respect to culture and those outside the building. And this is why local churches need to elevate technology to make it a priority, and church planting organizations, seminaries, and other institutions need to invest more in education and resources around tech-nology and future studies.

> **There is a day coming when church leaders won't feel the need to denigrate online church in order to raise up on-site church.**

"The next iteration isn't binary for sure. There will be many models, largely due to the inflection point society and culture has been forced into with the pandemic. The future of the church brings exciting opportunities. VR and the metaverse will challenge the requirement to be embodied together in the same phys-ical space. For example, holographic presence is closer than most think. And don't forget AI's impact on faith and religion—and there certainly will be an impact. So, for the future of the church, we need a better understanding of what parts of ministry life require corporate gatherings vs virtually mediated and asynchronous interactions. In the end, there is one thing that will continue to hold true: The Holy Spirit works in pixels too."

JON ACUFF
New York Times* bestselling author of seven books, including *Soundtracks: The Surprising Solution to Overthinking

"I think the future of the Church is hybrid. It's always going to be a both/and situation. Where churches get in trouble is when they over-focus on one or the other. Churches need to always have a virtual version because now there's an understanding that we can fit a few thousand people into a building, but we can fit 20K, 30K, 40K into a livestream space. Pastors will just have to understand that there's a lot of people they don't see who are being served by their church in ways they don't know."

KARA POWELL
Executive Director of Fuller Youth Institute and associate professor of Youth and Family Ministry

"Who is better positioned to understand what's going on in the world and culture, and where we're going to be five years from now than the young people in our churches? Thoughtful church leaders who want to know what the future will look like will spend more time with young people. Whether it's taking the same four young people out for coffee once a month to ask them questions, or sitting next to some young people in your church and asking them to show you what they are most excited about on their phones.

"I see church leaders looking for outside resources to help them with the digital church which is great, but we have experts in our midst. We have young people who, for the price of a cup of coffee, can give us some really good insights into what the future of the church may look like."

JP POKLUDA,
Lead Pastor at Harris Creek Baptist Church

"The most important thing churches should do is hold anything not commanded by the Scripture loosely. The Bible does not condemn campuses, streaming, or the use of technology. 1 Corinthians 9:19-23 casts a compelling vision for us to use whatever is available to us to reach as many people as possible. Technology will pave a way for Jesus' return. While it has a great potential for evil, it has an even greater potential for good! The invention of the printing press was met with much reluctance and resistance. The first book printed was the Bible. So, my 'what to do' is really a 'what not to do'; a warning. Do not be resistant to change. You have come to an understanding of the Gospel because someone was courageously innovative. I would suggest hiring someone who oversees this area, and increase their budget as you are able.

"I predict a return to the home church model, only with the use of TV streaming. Media rooms and living rooms will be 'church campuses'. Mega churches will still exist for some time, but most of their 'members' will not be there. It will be interesting to see how Virtual Reality and Augmented Reality evolve. I believe they will play a large role in this space one day, unless a greater technology arrives. Imagine the lady in Ready Player One who attends church by putting on her VR headset. We'll be there soon."

SLY KING
Social Media Coordinator at the
Worship Center Christian Church

"The church has to become intentional at watching technology and social media trends. This is an ever-changing landscape and the church has to become more focused on staying in step with the changes and not being years behind playing catch up. We need to be open to engaging with those who are outside of the church space for best practices and information on growing trends.

"I truly believe church will continue to evolve into a more engaging digital experience. The days of believing that the only door into the church is the physical door are over! I believe the online digital expression will become more interactive and feature virtual reality and augmented reality as well. There will be a hybrid approach to how we do church, and digital discipleship will take on a more engaging online approach that will allow those around the world to connect with the church and take the needed next steps in building their relationship with Christ. Lastly, the church needs to understand the digital space is always evolving, and be flexible!"

BRANDON DONALDSON
Senior Director of Church Partnerships,
Life.Church, and the first online pastor

"Here at YouVersion we have some axioms that help us align our product direction and decisions. One of those axioms is 'Mission First'. This axiom will go a long way for churches who are seeing many new technologies and wondering what they should do with them. Going to your mission first will always bring the right direction and decision. Every church will be a little different in the technologies they use and how they use them, but if they truly let the mission drive their decision, they will be in a great place. Then the question is not about where technology is going, but how technology can fulfill the mission. Mission always trumps method. Your mission always leads to the method. Churches should be focused on their mission and finding the momentum God is already bringing in their church. Then they can determine if and how technology could accelerate it.

"Too many times churches fear one of two things: First, they fear missing the big new technology so they jump in without strong consideration or strategy for their mission and their momentum. Second, they fear technology will take away from their mission and they stay away completely. This is an example of technology driving the discussion and decisions, but that will always be a bad position for technology. The mission and the momentum God is bringing should always drive the use of technology. Technology can't create momentum, but it can definitely help scale it and accelerate it."

PASTORSKAR
Twitch evangelist and founder of SKAR Ministries
"I'm a firm believer in thinking creatively and understanding that just because something has always been done a certain way, doesn't mean it's the only way to do it. Innovation is a beautiful thing and learning from each other and being willing to adapt allows us to go further and deeper than we ever could have before.

"People are spending so much time in these online spaces, if Christians and ministries aren't there intentionally too, then we're the only ones not represented. I seek to provide an alternative to the toxic content that is widespread, and instead, create something that can have an eternal impact by meeting people where they already are."

BEAU COFFRON
Social Media Director at Life.Church
"I think the church should start planning and budgeting now for a staff point person that can focus on innovation with new technology while at the same time working on connecting with people who move between online and offline attendance in services, small groups, etc. This staff position should start to become essential in a hybrid church environment."

CHAPTER 18 SO...WHAT'S NEXT?

JAY KRANDA
Online Pastor at Saddleback Church

"First, I believe that God uses new technology to accomplish his Kingdom goals. All throughout history God rides waves in generations, and technology is often one of those wave generators. Second, church leaders need to try out things without fully understanding them. The amazing thing with most technology is you can experiment with very little cost and commitment. Be a church that tries out new things and be willing to move on quickly if it doesn't work.

"The Church of the future will be more globally connected and deeply engaged because of technology. For sure, Sunday morning will be less relevant culturally, but new things will pop up that will be more engaging. I can't wait to see what God is going to bless next!"

BRADY SHEARER
Founder of Pro Church Tools

"I think the next iteration of church will be some kind of hybrid model of ministry. Prior to the pandemic, our churches were in a place of imbalance. For decades, we had over-indexed the 1-hour weekend service—to the neglect of the other 167 hours in a week. However, in the middle of the pandemic, we were also in a place of imbalance—just the inverse. We were forced to rely too heavily on digital outlets. Going forward, if we wish to serve our churches holistically, offline ministry and online ministry will need to exist in parallel, working in harmony, and understanding that neither can be a substitute for the other.

"Establishing a new metric for measuring effectiveness is the first and most important adjustment churches can make. Traditionally, we've used church attendance as our barometer for measuring life change—and understandably so, because quantifying life change and spiritual growth isn't easy. The thing is, church attendance only cares about external growth. Church attendance will only tell you if MORE people are attending your Sunday service this year compared to last year. In no way can church attendance offer any insight into internal growth at your church. Are the people already attending your church becoming more like Jesus? Church attendance can't measure that. So exchanging attendance for a metric like next steps is the first step to navigating the next decade—because if we can't properly evaluate our efforts, we're putting ourselves in a vulnerable place."

ALAN GEORGE
Pastor, leadership coach, digital strategist, and former Church Online Pastor at Life.Church

"It's almost impossible to predict what the future could look like. So rather than building strategies based on what I think could happen, I'd rather build a strategy based on what I know won't change. If we take time to think about it, we all can come up with things that we believe will stay the same. The two thoughts that come to my mind are:

1. The Word of God, the power of the Holy Spirit, and Biblical Community as a result of the Great Commission, should remain at the heart of who Christ's Church is and will be. So as you think about the future, leverage the advancements that are coming to build on what you know will remain.

2. In Matthew 9:38, Jesus asks us to pray to the Lord of the Harvest to send workers. God chooses to use people. So as the Church, let's continue to help grow, develop, and invest in leaders so that they are ready to step into the opportunities that tomorrow brings.

"As I read and hear about the technological advances that are in the works right now, anything seems possible. But through all of that, whether it's an immersive digital experience or a secret gathering in someone's basement, my prayer is that the Church continues to find its identity in who they are rather than where they meet. The Church is not a building, we are the Church."

HOLLY TATE
Senior Vice President of Growth, Leader

"The Church needs to have a culture of innovation. It's less about having the latest and greatest technology and more that you have a team culture that is ready to pivot and adapt to stay relevant with how people are convening online and offline. And offline will happen in small groups of tight knit communities."

JUSTIN PIERCY
Digital Strategy Director at Connexus Church
"The Church needs to move past its present digital/physical dichotomy mindset and embrace the mindset that digital experience and physical experience are part of a single, holistic whole."

TREY VAN CAMP
Lead Pastor at Passion Creek Church
"For me, growth isn't the primary goal for the Church—it's love. I want to love and serve as many people as possible and there's no greater reach than doing it online. In fact, a lot of what I have done hasn't directly grown my church, but it has helped advance the kingdom. And it has done much to grow my own soul.

"I hope to make space for God's grace in people's lives. Some of that is my live videos that teach Scripture and interact with the comments as I go. Another is my Tuesday morning prayers that empower people to pray two minutes at a time. It's also to lead my congregation to abstain from the digital world. I've been encouraging our folks to engage in silence, solitude, and sabbath. Much of that is only possible when we turn the digital world off."

STUART HALL
Director of Student Leadership for Orange
"Faith communities have to start with a brutal realization for many: technology is not going away. The vast majority of faith communities around the world are so far behind technologically because there seems to be a sense that technology is evil. So until we come to terms with the tech reality, tech will almost loom like this haunting apparition in our churches. In short, we cannot and will not be ready for the future because we are so far behind and resistant in most places.

"I think MetaChurch is the deal. We must abandon our ideas of what makes church 'biblical' because the context of the Church in the OT and NT were rooted more in social constructs than God mandates. I personally think that the faith communities that redefine what it means to worship corporately—meaning that it doesn't always have to involve singing and speaking but rather can mean time devoted to serve and build and care and dream—will be faith communities that flourish in the future. Faith communities can and should be about the work of making the kind of society where it is easier for people to be good.

"I wonder if a faith community that meets in homes several times a month, has a consistent presence of serving and building in their community every month, and perhaps has a once a month time of corporate worship will be the faith communities that become difference makers. That is what I believe will seem desirable to millennials and Gen Z-ers. But this shift will be monumental for a very viable reason: so many faith communities have placed so much equity in facilities, property, and gear. So to make this shift will mean rethinking how we think about tangible stuff."

JIM KEAT
Digital Minister at The Riverside Church, New York

"The church has always been called to embrace change. This is built into our DNA. This whole movement started with change (incarnation) and change (Pentecost) and change (Gentiles) and change (Constantine) and change (monastics) and change (the Reformation) and change. I'm a fan of 'ecclesia reformata sempre reformanda'—the Church is reformed and always being reformed. The Church needs to be true to who she has always been called to be—alive and active and present in the world around us. We can't look the way we always have in the past. To be a person of faith doesn't mean you have to be a person of antiquity. We need to be prepared for and ready to embrace (and cause?) change in the world and within the Church. If we don't, then we will always be one step, or one decade, behind.

"The next iteration of the Church will continue to be grounded in our local contexts but more connected to faith communities in the wider world. The Church will recognize that belonging extends beyond four walls as we engage sermons and speakers and faith formation content from around the world. It will embrace both physical and virtual experiences. After all, virtual is not the opposite of real. It's the opposite of physical. They are both real. This will create tension in what it means to be a 'local church' when we can have a global reach and impact. But that has always been the tension of the Church, now we're just all experiencing and exploring it all around us."

JEFF REED
**Director of Digital Church Planting at Stadia
Church Planting and Multi-Site**

"To move into the future, the Church needs to experiment more and empower people in the pews to be on mission. Right now, 75% of most church operating budgets goes to payroll and buildings, but we need to spend more money on other things than payroll and buildings. Staff and property are a lid to what God can do. If the Church is going to be successful in starting a movement, we need clarity on our objectives of disciple-making, and release control to our disciple-makers.

"The future of the Church is meta. There will not be one model, but lots of different models. Physical, digital, avatars, augmented, micro, workplace. The next iteration of church will be everything thrown in a blender and churches taking parts of different plans. This is what the future of the Church is. And I cannot wait."

WILLIAM VEST
Partner at RVRB Agency

"Church leaders must clarify and separate the methods and routines of the Church from the great commission that the Church is called to. It's easy to attach ourselves to things we have always done even if it is no longer the best way to carry out our calling. We need to use technology to amplify the message in order to more effectively carry out the great commission. In contrast, when technology gets in the way of effectively carrying out the great commission we must remove it. In order to steward our calling well, we must determine the best paths to get there.

"As teaching continues to decentralize and scale larger through technology, I believe the true community that Christ calls us to within the Church will centralize in communities and scale down into smaller groups of people. I think the idea of 'church' will change from a Sunday teaching to a smaller group meeting in many people's minds."

TYLER SANSOM
Pastor at Church Anywhere

"The Church was always a place where innovation happened. The great artists were commissioned by the Church. Great composers wrote beautiful compositions for the Church. But then, at some point in the 20th century, the Church stopped innovating and started having to play catch up to society. We have to not only embrace new technologies and new ways to reach people for the Gospel, but we have to be on the forefront of helping create those new avenues. God is the ultimate Creator, and he has given us that creative trait. It is time for us to push into that."

DAN SCOTT
Orange Director of Elementary Strategy

"While making any sort of prediction about the future of the Church feels like a shot in the dark, that doesn't mean we can't take cues from what the emerging generations value. If the Church wants continued influence in the culture, it will need to put people over programming, group relationships over stage personalities, and authenticity over polish. The Church will engage online life as much, if not more, than life in-person. Events and services will integrate unique online and off-line experiences to provide both a real-time and on-demand experience for more people to connect with the Church. With a shift in perspective, the Church could lead the way in how culture innovates in this space.

"More than ever, the Church needs an open-handed approach to how to create ministry opportunities—including how we define church attendance, how we program services and events, and how we engage the emerging generations. The Church must recognize that how the world connects with content has officially changed and will continue to morph in step with technological advancements. We shouldn't be scared of the technology, but see it as a tool to further Jesus' great commission. However, when it comes to our local iteration of church programs, all of it should be planned with agility in mind. Being able to adapt quickly will be a crucial mark of the Church's ability to have influence with future generations."

SEAN CANNELL
CEO of Think Media

"The Church needs to remember that the message doesn't change but the methods do. Churches that are overly romantic about how church was done yesterday will miss out on what the Church will look like tomorrow. That's why church leaders need to stay orthodox in their theology but open minded in their strategy for reaching and impacting culture. Embracing technology means getting educated on where people are, and how they are spending their time and attention, which includes social media, the Internet, Blockchain, and NFTs. While some of these things are bleeding edge right now, they'll be here sooner than we realize and church leaders need to be ready. Additionally, a pandemic has taught us that churches have to embrace live streaming, online campuses, and digital ministry. And while it may not be ideal, and it certainly doesn't replace the in-person gathering, we've learned that it was absolutely necessary and could be more so in the future. Churches that ignore this will, at best, lose relevance and, at worst, have to close their doors.

"The great Christian revivalist, Charles Finney, said preachers need 'the Bible in one hand, and the map of the human mind in the other', because every pastor should have theological understanding of the Bible, and know how to reach humans, and that is so true today! Church leaders are called to communicate the Good News, therefore it's encumbered on them to not only continuously work on becoming better communicators, but to embrace new mediums of communication."

"I think the next version of Church will include communicating the gospel message in new modalities, which will include short form video, interactive storytelling, live streaming, social media, and as bizarre as it sounds now, VR and AR environments. While much of the church will be critical of things like Facebook creating the metaverse, pioneering church leaders will embrace it like Paul, who became all things to all people in order to win some. We will see churches planted in the metaverse that will reach people, share the Gospel message, and see people won for the Kingdom of God, while rigid and religious critics will sit on the sidelines misquoting Scripture as to why that should not be happening."

DJ CHUANG
**Digital strategy consultant and
author of MultiAsian.Church**

"We are already seeing and experiencing the next iteration of the Church during this post-pandemic season. Churches will look smaller in size—like house churches and localized neighborhood groups—and they'll be more adept with using digital technologies to augment their spirituality. Escalating costs of staffing and facilities are drastically reshaping churches to focus back to the essentials of making disciples rather than producing programs."

TONI COLLIER
Author, speaker, and Founder of Broken Crayons

"The Church has been going through a period of pruning and refining, and I personally think that is okay because we're now defining the people who inhabit the Church, and not just the church building. When we look at the Acts 2 Church, we see this group of people who not only dwelled in the Temple courts, but outside of the Temple courts. In fact, one of the first miracles done by the disciples was in front of 'the church' and not in it. And we see that the people were also gathering in their homes. So, my hope is that we will raise up a generation that would gather wherever they are—in professional spaces, in counseling spaces, on sports fields and in academia—and would say that 'this is the church and we will dwell here'. We need to be a Church that will proclaim the name of Jesus outside of the four walls of the building."

TOM KANG
Lead Pastor of NewStory Church

"Remember when trying to find your future spouse through online dating was that weird, new, thing? Fast forward about two decades later, and now half the couples you know have met online. I think the next iteration of church looks like that. The pandemic necessitated and normalized church online. It's no longer weird. No longer fringe. And the sooner we leverage the realities and innovations of church online with the innate desires in each of us for in-person community ... the closer we step towards our 'happily ever after.'"

KATIE ALLRED
CEO ChurchCommunications.com
"The future of the Church is small and includes some form of online community. We've created big buildings and big programs but God has called us to one-on-one discipleship and mentoring. He has called us to worship together and it can look different than before. We might gather online, we might gather in the metaverse, but the point is we're still gathering, learning, and growing together as one body."

PAULA DANNIELLE
Pastor, communicator, and Next Gen Ministry Coach
"The impact of the Church has always depended on her ability to reach people with the truth of the Gospel through methods in which they could receive it. I think the Church, with the next generation of leaders, will be known for how they are engaging the public more than what happens in private. The Church will be identified for what they do and do not say on social media platforms. The Church will be known for how it addresses or ignores the people that systems disregard. I believe the 'ekklesia'—those who profess to follow Jesus—will be characterized by how we show up in the world rather than where we meet. In this next iteration of church, we will be known for our actions that draw people into experiences that exhibit the love of Christ."

JASON MORRIS
Global Innovation Pastor at Westside Family Church
"I think the next iteration of Church will look more like the first one using tech. Because technology removes barriers, it's giving us the freedom to conceive of the church in the way we find it in the book of Acts, where the Church expressed itself as a decentralized network of small gatherings in homes and public spaces meeting daily for encouragement, togetherness, and love, with the liturgy of those gatherings being guided by what we find in 1 Corinthians 14, instead of what we were practically able to do for the past few centuries. We have more tools now to express that Acts 2 Church than we ever had.

"I'm seeing new churches that are starting and maintaining relationships digitally while discovering new rhythms and forms of gathering. Think daily and quarterly more than weekly. The next iteration of

Church is very intentional about using the strengths of each tool God has given us. Digital tools for content delivery, social tools for daily connectedness, and intentionally using physical gatherings to relate to each other in ways that tech will never do. Each tool and environment will be used for what it does best—creating a mixture that will allow more people to become full participants in Jesus' Church instead of spectators!"

TIM LUCAS
Lead Pastor at Liquid Church, New Jersey

"We launched Liquid Church in 2007—the same year the first iPhone came out. I distinctly remember the Sunday service when I said to our congregation, "Open your Bibles ..." and more blue screens lit up than pages turned. That was the moment I realized the tech in catechism was here to stay. We never looked back. Our first Church Online Pastor Dave Adamson pioneered our early efforts in digital discipleship—streaming services, hosting virtual groups, and architecting social strategies for believers who felt at home at Liquid, but would never step foot in our physical building.

"I'll never forget when Pastor Dave organized a Zoom baptism in someone's backyard pool 6,000 miles away for friends in our online congregation. Who knew the Holy Spirit could flow through pixels? Ever since, Liquid has intentionally taken a fluid approach to ensure our church is ready for technological advances yet to be invented. Liquid, like water, is fluid and flexible—adapting to the shape of any container. So our ministry team makes a careful distinction between the content and our containers. The content of our message (the Gospel of Jesus Christ) never changes; but the containers that carry it must always evolve—like digital wineskins—to engage the hearts and minds of the next generation."

ALANA SHARP
Social Media Director for Church of the Highlands

"I believe that the Church should stay relevant and prepare for the technological advances that will inevitably come. With the way technology is advancing so quickly, flexibility is key. We can stay true to our vision while being adaptable on how we fulfill it! I believe we should have a plan to financially prepare for infrastructure changes and to stay up to speed on the latest developments in order to remain relevant and attractive.

"Online church will continue to be needed as it may be the only way some people are comfortable approaching the church. I think that there will be discipleship plans to help an online audience take next steps and fulfill their purpose. I also believe that we need to find new ways to continue making in-person churches more attractive in order to show people the beauty they can find in gathering together with the Body of Christ!"

* * *

These are some incredibly helpful thoughts from some smart friends with decades of experience in ministry—and I agree with all of them!

GLOSSARY OF TERMS

B-roll — A video editing term to identify any video footage that is supplemental or alternative to the main or primary footage.

Click-through rate (CTR) — A metric on YouTube that tracks how often viewers watched a video after seeing a thumbnail or video title.

Cutaways — A shot that "cuts away" from the main content in order to add additional information or context. A cutaway is typically followed by a cut back to the main video content.

Cyberbullying — The use of technology to harass, threaten, embarrass, or target another person.

Full screen slides — A static screen containing written or visual information that takes in the entire frame of a video, and acts as a pattern interruption to the main content.

Jump cuts — A single shot that is broken with a cut that makes the subject in the video appear closer to the camera. In a jump cut, the camera position does not change, the frame size is simply increased during the editing process.

Keyword and keyphrase — A digital marketing term to describe a word or a group of words a person uses to perform a search in a search engine.

Keyword description — A video description that helps YouTube understand and contextualize the content of a video. Descriptions that are well optimized can lead to higher rankings in YouTube search by helping the platform identify your target audience. Two hundred to 300 words is the ideal length of a YouTube description in order to provide the platform with enough information on the video content, however YouTube recommends you emphasize keywords in the first two to three sentences, and "put the most important keywords toward the beginning of your description."

Keyword tail — A keyword tail is a specific phrase generally made from three to five words that are more specific than generic terms, generating a smaller number of searches within a niche.

Megachurch — A church, usually Protestant, with a very large congregation (over 2000), typically housed in a complex offering sophisticated multimedia presentations and a range of secular facilities and services.

MetaChurch — A group of Jesus followers who worship God and learn about their faith in a church building, a small group, house Bible study, through video on-demand, podcast, or a live-streamed service who still constitute one "congregation."

Pattern interruption — Any visual or audio change in a video that refocuses a viewer's attention.

Search Engine Results Page (SERP) — The page displayed by Google, Yahoo, or any other search engine after you enter a query into the search bar.

Slash-cam — An abbreviation for slash camera, a camera that is positioned diagonally to the subject in the video. This camera is typically used to capture cutaways to help in the editing process.

SOPs — Short for Standard Operating Procedures, which are a list of step-by-step instructions to help staff and volunteers perform routine operations.

Stinger — A short video designed to call a viewer's attention to a new section of video content. Also referred to as a bumper.

Thumbnail — A still image that acts as the preview image or cover photo for your video. After you upload a video, YouTube automatically generates three options, or you can upload your own custom thumbnail if your account is verified.

Video hook — An interesting element at the very beginning of a video that draws in viewers.

View duration — The total watch time of a video, divided by the total number of video plays, including replays. This metric measures your video's ability to engage viewers.

Watch time — The total amount of time viewers have spent watching a video.

YouTube cards — Interactive elements that act as clickable calls to action used to promote videos, playlists, websites, or channels. YouTube cards appear on videos viewed on both desktop and mobile videos.

YouTube channel tags — Keywords and keyphrases that highlight your channel and content. They are an essential part of making your channel discoverable.

YouTube Creator Academy — A free online training program offered by Youtube to help creators get the most from their YouTube channel.

YouTube end screen — A YouTube platform feature that appears in the last 5–20 seconds of a video. The end screen can be either a thumbnail or a video, which is used as a backdrop for YouTubers to promote videos, playlists, and subscriptions. Also called end cards.

YouTube Playlist — A collection of videos grouped together on a YouTube Channel. Playlists are managed in YouTube Studio, and can be used to gather together videos with similar themes, styles, or topics.

YouTube Studio — The channel hub for YouTube Creators to manage their YouTube channel. It was formerly known as Creator Studio.

YouTube subscribers — Someone who has chosen to "follow" your channel and your content so they can stay updated with your latest videos.

YouTube video velocity — Tracks how quickly a specific video is getting organic views on YouTube. The faster a video gets views from the moment it is published, the more that video is promoted to new viewers.

YouTube views — Tracks the number of legitimate, audience initiated views for your videos. More views indicates the overall success of a video's content.

Zero Moment Of Truth — A Google term for the moment a consumer researches a brand or product online.

ENDNOTES

1. https://1.bp.blogspot.com/-kvjGhmo3U3o/YVsI7Z3DtDI/ AAAAAAAA0DA/LMLELkg2jxA7JuPPL9CBiYja5etTM7_YQCL-cBGAsYHQ/s600/-4-Church-Social-Media-Managers-Face-book.png

2. Karen Weise, *"Amazon's profit soars 220 percent as pandemic drives shopping online,"* New York Times, April 29, 2021, updated May 12, 2021. https://www.nytimes.com/2021/04/29/technology/amazons-profits-triple.html

3. Rohit Arora, *Which Companies Did Well During The Coronavirus Pandemic?* Forbes.com, June 30, 2020. https://www.forbes.com/sites/rohitarora/2020/06/30/which-companies-did-well-during-the-coronavirus-pandemic/?sh=7a9688a97409

4. Paul Ziobro, *These Businesses Thrived in Lockdown. Can They Keep It Up Now?* The Wall Street Journal, March 10, 2021. https://www.wsj.com/articles/for-doordash-etsy-and-others-next-test-is-sustaining-pandemic-growth-11615384800

5. Rohit Arora, *Which Companies Did Well During The Coronavirus Pandemic?* Forbes.com, June 30, 2020. https://www.forbes.com/sites/rohitarora/2020/06/30/which-companies-did-well-during-the-coronavirus-pandemic/?sh=7a9688a97409

6. Christo Petrov, *50 Alarming Cyberbullying Statistics for 2021,* techjury.com, January 4, 2022. https://techjury.net/blog/cyberbullying-statistics/#gref

7. *In U.S., Decline of Christianity Continues at Rapid Pace*, Pew Research Center, October 17, 2019. https://www.pewforum.org/2019/10/17/in-u-s-decline-of-christianity-continues-at-rapid-pace/

8. *Signs of Decline & Hope Among Key Metrics of Faith*, Barna.com, March 4, 2020. https://www.barna.com/research/changing-state-of-the-church/

9. *How often do you attend church or synagogue - at least once a week, almost every week, about once a month, seldom, or never?*, statista.com, https://www.statista.com/statistics/245491/church-attendance-of-americans/

10. *Do Americans Replace Traditional Church with Digital Faith Expressions?* Barna.com, March 12, 2020. https://www.barna.com/research/worship-shifting/

11. *What's on the Minds of America's Pastors?* barna.com, February 3, 2020. https://www.barna.com/research/whats_on_mind_americas_pastors/?utm_source=Newsletter&utm_medium=email&utm_content=Barna+Update%3A+Pastors+Rank+Top+Concerns+Facing+the+U+S++Church&utm_campaign=Pastors++Concerns+BU+%282%2F6%29

12. *What's Worrying Pastors Most? Barna Group to Release "State of the Church 2020,"* Missions Box, February 14, 2020. https://missionsbox.org/news/whats-worrying-pastors-most-barna-group-to-release-state-of-the-church-2020/

13. *The Facebook Files: A Wall Street Journal investigation*, The Wall Street Journal, October 1, 2021. https://www.wsj.com/articles/the-facebook-files-11631713039?mod=e2tw

14. *Instagram for kids paused after backlash*, BBC News, 27 September 2021. https://www.bbc.com/news/technology-58707753

15. Andrew Hutchinson, *Instagram Pauses 'Instagram for Kids' Project After Recent Media Reports*, Social Media Today, September 27, 2021. https://www.socialmediatoday.com/news/instagram-pauses-instagram-for-kids-project-after-recent-media-reports/607243/

16. Georgia Wells, Jeff Horwitz, and Deepa Seetharaman, *Facebook Knows Instagram Is Toxic for Teen Girls, Company Documents Show*, The Wall Street Journal, September 14, 2021. https://www.wsj.com/articles/facebook-knows-instagram-is-toxic-for-teen-girls-company-documents-show-11631620739?mod=hp_lead_pos7&mod=article_inline

17. *Facebook Files: 5 things leaked documents reveal*, BBC.com, September 14, 2021. https://www.bbc.com/news/technology-58678332

18. *Pornography Statistics*, covenanteyes.com. https://www.covenanteyes.com/pornstats/

19. *20 Must-Know Stats About The Porn Industry And Its Underage Consumers*, fightthenewdrug.org, October 8, 2021. https://fightthenewdrug.org/10-porn-stats-that-will-blow-your-mind/

20. Jim Waterson, *Half of adults in UK watched porn during pandemic, says Ofcom*, The Guardian, June 9, 2021. https://www.theguardian.com/media/2021/jun/09/half-british-adults-watched-porn-pandemic-ofcom#:~:text=Half%20the%20adult%20population%20of,adult%20material%20in%20September%202020

21. https://www.instagram.com/p/CZK8LEoF7JI/

22. *Young adults around the world are less religious by several measures*, Pew Research Center, June 13, 2018. https://www.pewforum.org/2018/06/13/young-adults-around-the-world-are-less-religious-by-several-measures/

23. Jeffery M Jones, *Church Membership Falls Below Majority for First Time*, news.gallup.com, March 29, 2021. https://news.gallup.com/poll/341963/church-membership-falls-be-low-majority-first-time.aspx

24. Joseph Choi, *U.S. church membership falls below 50 percent for first time: poll*, The Hill, March 29, 2021. https://thehill.com/homenews/media/545364-us-church-membership-falls-below-50-percent-for-first-time-poll

25. Neil Saunders, *How Home Depot Became the Online Leader in a Difficult Product Category*, onespace.com. https://www.onespace.com/blog/2017/11/how-home-depot-became-the-online-leader-in-a-difficult-product-category/

26. Pamela N. Danziger, *Home Depot's Transformation To A Fully Interconnected Retailer Shows Record-Breaking Results*, Forbes, February 26, 2020. https://www.forbes.com/sites/pamdanziger/2020/02/26/home-depots-transforma-tion-to-a-fully-interconnected-retailer-shows-record-break-ing-results/?sh=45d661e73307

27. Pamela N. Danziger, *Home Depot's Transformation To A Fully Interconnected Retailer Shows Record-Breaking Results*, Forbes.com, February 26, 2020. https://www.forbes.com/sites/pamdanziger/2020/02/26/home-depots-transforma-tion-to-a-fully-interconnected-retailer-shows-record-break-ing-results/?sh=6072da9f7330

28. Jim Lecinski, ZMOT: *Why It Matters Now More Than Ever*, Think With Google, August 2014. https://www.thinkwithgoogle.com/marketing-strategies/search/zmot-why-it-matters-now-more-than-ever/

29. *Screens, man's new best friend*, mainstreet.com.au, September 28, 2020. https://mainstreetinsights.com.au/screens-mans-new-best-friend/

30. Anna Patty, *The meaning of life: Australians praying more during COVID-19*, The Sydney Morning Herald, August 23, 2020. https://www.smh.com.au/national/the-meaning-of-life-australians-praying-more-during-covid-19-20200820-p55nla.html

31. *The impact of COVID-19 on relationships and spirituality*, mccrindle.com.au. https://mccrindle.com.au/insights/blog/the-impact-of-covid-19-on-relationships-and-spirituality/

32. *38% of U.S. Pastors Have Thought About Quitting Full-Time Ministry in the Past Year*, Barna.com, November 16, 2021. https://www.barna.com/research/pastors-well-being/?utm_source=Newsletter&utm_medium=email&utm_content=Barna+Update%3A+38++of+U+S++Pastors+Have+Thought+About+Quitting+Full-Time+Ministry+in+the+Past+Year&utm_campaign=2021-11-24_Pastor+Burnout_BU_RESEND

33. CollinsDictionary.com. https://www.collinsdictionary.com/dictionary/english/megachurch

34. Thom S. Rainer, *What Megachurches, Neighborhood Churches, and the Multi-Site Movement Are Telling Us*, ChurchAnswers.com, April 19, 2021. https://churchanswers.com/blog/what-megachurches-neighborhood-churches-and-the-multi-site-movement-are-telling-us/

35. *Life in U.S. Religious Congregations Slowly Edges Back Toward Normal*, Pew Research Center, March 22, 2021. https://www.pewforum.org/2021/03/22/life-in-u-s-religious-congregations-slowly-edges-back-toward-normal/

36. Megan Brenan, *In-Person Religious Service Attendance Is Rebounding*, news.gallup.com, June 2, 2021. https://news.gallup.com/poll/350462/person-religious-service-attendance-rebounding.aspx

37. Pamela N. Danziger, *Home Depot's Transformation To A Fully Interconnected Retailer Shows Record-Breaking Results*, Forbes.com, February 26, 2020. https://www.forbes.com/sites/pamdanziger/2020/02/26/home-depots-transformation-to-a-fully-interconnected-retailer-shows-record-breaking-results/?sh=45d661e73307

38. *ChurchPulse Weekly Podcast: Mark Batterson on Pastoring in a Digital Age, Part 1*, Barna.com, August 26, 2020. https://www.barna.com/research/mark-batterson-part-1/

39. *ChurchPulse Weekly Podcast: Mark Batterson on Pastoring in a Digital Age, Part 2*, Barna.com, September 1, 2020. https://www.barna.com/research/mark-batterson-part-2/

40. https://careynieuwhof.com/online-church-engagement-summit/

41. *Do Americans Replace Traditional Church with Digital Faith Expressions?* Barna.com, March 12, 2020. https://www.barna.com/research/worship-shifting/

42. *Do Americans Replace Traditional Church with Digital Faith Expressions?* Barna.com, March 12, 2020. https://www.barna.com/research/worship-shifting/

43. Diana Aguilera, *The Truth About Online Lying Are we more honest online? It depends*, Stanford Magazine, September 2018. https://stanfordmag.org/contents/the-truth-about-online-lying

44. *Six Questions About the Future of the Hybrid Church Experience*, Barna Group, 2020, page 39

45. Alan George, *Discipleship For A Digital Age*, 2021, page 34

46. *Most popular social networks worldwide as of October 2021, ranked by number of active users*, Statista.com, January 28, 2022. https://www.statista.com/statistics/272014/global-social-networks-ranked-by-number-of-users/

47. Brooke Auxier and Monica Anderson, *Social Media Use in 2021 A majority of Americans say they use YouTube and Facebook, while use of Instagram, Snapchat and TikTok is especially common among adults under 30*, Pew Research Center, April 7, 2021. https://www.pewresearch.org/Internet/2021/04/07/social-media-use-in-2021/#:~:text=Additionally%2C%20a%20vast%20majority%20of,among%20those%2065%20and%20older

48. Emma Bazilian, *Infographic: 50% of Gen Z 'Can't Live Without YouTube' and Other Stats That Will Make You Feel Old*, AdWeek, May 21, 2017. https://www.adweek.com/performance-marketing/infographic-50-of-gen-z-cant-live-without-youtube-and-other-stats-that-will-make-you-feel-old/

49. David Mogensen, *I want-to-do moments: From home to beauty*, Think with Google, May 2015. https://www.thinkwithgoogle.com/consumer-insights/consumer-trends/i-want-to-do-micro-moments/

50. Martin Armstrong, *YouTube is Responsible for 37% of All Mobile Internet Traffic*, Statista.com, March 11, 2019. https://www.statista.com/chart/17321/global-downstream-mobile-traffic-by-app

51. John Gramlich, *10 facts about Americans and Facebook*, Pew Research Center, June 1, 2021. https://www.pewresearch.org/fact-tank/2021/06/01/facts-about-americans-and-facebook/

52. Amy Watson, *Religious books sales revenue in the United States from 2017 to 2020*, Statista.com, June 24, 2021. https://www.statista.com/statistics/251467/religious-books-sales-revenue-in-the-us/

53. Fish4Ever, *Teaching my Fish How to Play Basketball | Fish Tricks #1*, August 14, 2020. https://youtu.be/wQ7AgP2ThX8

54. *Watch how to add a custom video thumbnail*, Creator Academy, https://creatoracademy.youtube.com/page/lesson/thumbnails

55. David Shiffman, *How to Create Video Thumbnails That Boost Views*, Social Media Examiner, June 8, 2015. https://www.socialmediaexaminer.com/create-video-thumbnails-that-boost-views/

56. *72% of popular thumbnails on YouTube feature a human face, and attract more views*, YouGov America, November 4, 2020. https://today.yougov.com/topics/resources/articles-reports/2020/11/03/72-popular-thumbnails-youtube-feature-human-face-a

57. Brian Dean, *We Analyzed 1.3 million YouTube Videos, Here's What We Learned About YouTube SEO*, BackLinko.com, February 28, 2017. https://backlinko.com/youtube-ranking-factors

58. Nick Nelson, *The Power of a Picture*, netflix.com, May 3, 2016. https://about.netflix.com/en/news/the-power-of-a-picture

59. Anne Trafton, *In the blink of an eye: MIT neuroscientists find the brain can identify images seen for as little as 13 milliseconds*, MIT News, January 16, 2014. https://news.mit.edu/2014/in-the-blink-of-an-eye-0116

60. David Crary, *How long is the sermon? Study ranks Christian churches*, AP News, December 17, 2019. https://apnews.com/article/us-news-ap-top-news-religion-christianity-d5c3a0bd7726f18d5cff44efa1bd4cfd

61. *The Best Video Length for Different Videos on YouTube*, minimatters.com, March 11, 2014. https://www.minimatters.com/youtube-best-video-length/

62. L. Ceci, *Average YouTube video length as of December 2018, by category*, Statistica.com, August 23, 2021. https://www.statista.com/statistics/1026923/youtube-video-category-average-length/

63. Carey Nieuwhof, *The Real Competition for the Local Church*, Outreach Magazine, November 6, 2020. https://outreach-magazine.com/features/leadership/61105-the-real-competition-for-the-local-church.html

64. *Use square and vertical video to engage mobile customers*, Google Ads Help. https://support.google.com/google-ads/answer/9128498?hl=en-AU

65. *TED Talks Daily*, https://podcasts.apple.com/us/podcast/ted-talks-daily/id160904630

66. *TEDx Shorts*, https://www.ted.com/podcasts/tedxshorts

67. *NPR News Now*, https://www.npr.org/podcasts/500005/npr-news-now

68. *Loneliness doubles in Europe during the pandemic*, EU Science Hub, July 26, 2021. https://ec.europa.eu/jrc/en/news/new-report-loneliness-doubles-europe-during-pandemic

69. Elena Renken, *Most Americans Are Lonely, And Our Workplace Culture May Not Be Helping*, NPR, January 23, 2020. https://www.npr.org/sections/health-shots/2020/01/23/798676465/most-americans-are-lonely-and-our-workplace-culture-may-not-be-helping

70. *Loneliness is at Epidemic Levels in America*, newsroom.cigna.com, January 2020. https://newsroom.cigna.com/loneliness-in-america

71. *Loneliness and the Workplace*, newsroom.cigna.com, January 2020. https://www.cigna.com/static/www-cigna-com/docs/about-us/newsroom/studies-and-reports/combatting-loneliness/cigna-2020-loneliness-factsheet.pdf

72. *Social isolation and loneliness*, Australian Institute of Health and Welfare, September 16, 2021. https://www.aihw.gov.au/reports/australias-welfare/social-isolation-and-loneliness-covid-pandemic

73. Kayla Osborne, *Informer: Not feeling so festive? Remember you aren't alone*, Northern Beaches Review, December 7, 2021. https://www.northernbeachesreview.com.au/story/7541771/not-feeling-so-festive-remember-you-arent-alone/

74. *Social isolation and loneliness*, Australian Institute of Health and Welfare, September 16, 2021. https://www.aihw.gov.au/reports/australias-welfare/social-isolation-and-loneliness-covid-pandemic

75. Jana Riess, *Study: Gen Z didn't hear from faith leaders during the pandemic. But they didn't lose their faith either*, America Magazine, June 2, 2021. https://www.americamagazine.org/faith/2021/06/02/gen-z-faith-community-study-covid-19-240776

76. *The New Normal: 8 Ways to Care for Gen Z in a PostPandemic World*, Springtide Research Institute, April 2021. https://www.springtideresearch.org/wp-content/uploads/2021/04/the-newnormal-pr.pdf

77. Patricia Duchene, *The Science Behind Pattern Interrupt*, Forbes.com, July 17, 2020. https://www.forbes.com/sites/patriciaduchene/2020/07/17/the-science-behind-pattern-interrupt/?sh=3f05e1d04207

78. Carmine Gallo, *Talk Like Ted: The 9 Public-Speaking Secrets of the World's Top Minds*, page 190, Pan Macmillan, March 2014.

79. Chris Agar, *How Much In The Heights Cost to Make Compared To Disney+'s Hamilton*, ScreenRant, June 10, 2021. https://screenrant.com/in-heights-movie-budget-cost-hamilton-musical-comparison/#:~:text=Disney%20paid%20%2475%20million%20for,granted%20a%20%2412.5%20million%20budget

80. Carey Nieuwhof, *Why Attending Church No Longer Makes Sense*, careynieuwhof.com. https://careynieuwhof.com/why-attending-church-no-longer-makes-sense/

81. Lia Eustachewich, *The one place you can still find a Blockbuster*, New York Post, April 24, 2017. https://nypost.com/2017/04/24/the-one-place-you-can-still-find-a-blockbuster/

82. Minda Zetlin, *Blockbuster Could Have Bought Netflix for $50 Million, but the CEO Thought It Was a Joke*, inc.com, September 20, 2019. https://www.inc.com/minda-zetlin/netflix-blockbuster-meeting-marc-randolph-reed-hastings-john-antioco.html

83. Greg Satell, *A Look Back At Why Blockbuster Really Failed And Why It Didn't Have To*, Forbes.com, September 5, 2014. https://www.forbes.com/sites/gregsatell/2014/09/05/a-look-back-at-why-blockbuster-really-failed-and-why-it-didnt-have-to/?sh=482e5f341d64

84. Bethany Biron, *The last remaining Blockbuster on Earth will be listed on Airbnb for a limited time in September at just $4 per night. Take a look inside*, Business Insider Australia, August 12, 2020. https://www.businessinsider.com.au/blockbuster-is-renting-last-location-in-the-world-on-airbnb-2020-8

85. Andy Ash, *The rise and fall of Blockbuster and how it's surviving with just one store left*, Business Insider Australia, January 16, 2020. https://www.businessinsider.com.au/the-rise-and-fall-of-blockbuster-video-streaming-2020-1?r=US&IR=T

86. *Audio and Podcasting Fact Sheet*, Pew Research Center, June 29, 2021. https://www.pewresearch.org/journalism/fact-sheet/audio-and-podcasting/

87. *2021 Global Podcast Statistics, Demographics & Habits*, PodcastHosting.org, April 10, 2021. https://podcasthosting.org/podcast-statistics/

88. Marie Charlotte Götting, *Leading podcast genres in the United States in October 2020*, Statista.com, October 14, 2021. https://www.statista.com/statistics/786938/top-podcast-genres/

89. *Podcast Stats Soundbite: 3 Surprising Stats about Religious Podcasts*, Blubrry.com, January 14, 2019. https://blubrry.com/podcast-insider/2019/01/14/3-surprising-podcast-stats-religious/

90. *Why Run an Alpha: Alpha and the Local Church.* https://static1.squarespace.com/static/534b-f89be4b09ed6294bf7dd/t/5b715940032be-42d141171ab/1534155122963/Why+Run+Alpha.pdf

91. Carey Nieuwhof Leadership Podcast episode 466. https://careynieuwhof.com/wp-content/uploads/2020/05/CNLP_343-%E2%80%93With_Nicky-Gumbel.pdf

92. Anne Lim, *Thousands Seek Answers Online Through Alpha*, Eternity News, August 11, 2021. https://www.eternitynews.com.au/australia/thousands-seek-answers-online-through-alpha/

93. Carey Nieuwhof Leadership Podcast episode 334. https://careynieuwhof.com/wp-content/uploads/2020/04/CNLP_334-%E2%80%93With_Mark-Sayers.pdf

94. https://influencers.church/zoomchurch/

95. *2 in 5 Churchgoers Are Open to Inviting Others to Digital Church Services*, Barna.com, December 2, 2020. https://www.barna.com/research/digital-service-invitation/

96. Jon Simpson, *Finding Brand Success In The Digital World*, Forbes.com, August 25, 2017. https://www.forbes.com/sites/forbesagencycouncil/2017/08/25/finding-brand-success-in-the-digital-world/?sh=1d68f2a3626e

97. Brian Dean, *Twitch Usage and Growth Statistics: How Many People Use Twitch in 2022?* Backlinko.com, January 5, 2022. https://backlinko.com/twitch-users

98. Dave Adamson, *Church as we know it is over. Here's what's next*, foxnews.com, March 11, 2019. https://www.foxnews.com/opinion/churches-as-we-know-it-are-over-here-is-how-to-engage-the-faithful

99. *Bobby Gruenewald: Tech, YouVersion, Resources, & You (Part I)*, ChurchMag.com, May 17, 2020. https://churchm.ag/bobby-gruenewald-tech-youversion-resources-you-part-i-podcast-307/

100. Teodora Dobrilova, *35+ Must-Know SMS Marketing Statistics in 2021*, TechJury.com, January 4, 2022. https://techjury.net/blog/sms-marketing-statistics/#gref

101. Andrew Hutchinson, *TikTok Leads Christmas Day Download Charts, New Markers of the Coming Metaverse Shift,* Social Media Today, December 28, 2021. https://www.socialmediatoday.com/news/tiktok-leads-christmas-day-download-charts-new-markers-of-the-coming-metav/616570/?fbclid=IwAR3mCv1GKvf6TnFe-B6Lcwxr78IfkXxl2QQQ8sVs9JwL_b1ayR4iKK6wpcqU

102. Jonathan Merritt, *Is AI a Threat to Christianity? Are you there, God? It's I, robot*, The Atlantic, February 3, 2017. https://www.theatlantic.com/technology/archive/2017/02/artificial-intelligence-christianity/515463/

103. Sigal Samuel, *Robot priests can bless you, advise you, and even perform your funeral*, VOX, January 13, 2020. https://www.vox.com/future-perfect/2019/9/9/20851753/ai-religion-robot-priest-mindar-buddhism-christianity

104. *Creators of the YouVersion Bible App celebrate launch of new app, Bible Lens*, AP News, August 6, 2018. https://apnews.com/press-release/pr-globenewswire/f0cd38b9c81f7499fa4f4143d5187577

105. Jon A Vickers, *Field preaching*, A Dictionary of Methodism in Britain and Ireland. https://dmbi.online/index.php?do=app.entry&id=1025

106. *Wesley Begins Field-preaching*, ccel.org. https://www.ccel.org/ccel/wesley/journal.vi.iii.i.html

107. Andrew Hutchinson, *TikTok Leads Christmas Day Download Charts, New Markers of the Coming Metaverse Shift, Social Media Today*, December 28, 2021. https://www.socialmediatoday.com/news/tiktok-leads-christmas-day-download-charts-new-markers-of-the-coming-metav/616570/?fbclid=IwAR3mCv1GKvf6TnFe-B6Lcwxr78IfkXxl2QQQ8sVs9JwL_b1ayR4iKK6wpcqU

108. https://www.youtube.com/watch?v=9DEeMG_Gidw

ACKNOWLEDGEMENTS

THERE'S A HANDFUL OF PEOPLE who helped make this book possible. Through their time, wisdom, expertise, forethought, and general encouragement, this book has gone from my brain to the page or tablet . . . or whatever.

The first shout out has to go to my family—my wife, Meg, and our daughters, Chelsea, Ella, and Jordyn. Not only did they put up with me being away for days on a writing retreat, or locked away in my office busily writing and rewriting this book, their willingness to move to the other side of the world in 2008 made it possible for me to become an online and social media pastor in the first place. And their willingness to move from New Jersey to Atlanta (arguably a bigger cultural shift than moving from Melbourne to New Jersey) allowed me to further expand my experience in digital ministry. Lovey, I wouldn't be alive without your patience and encouragement. Girls, I love you 9000 (that's 3000 each)!

Two people made this book readable. Like seriously.

Sarah Anderson turned my chicken scrawl, bullet points, random ideas, frustrations, social media posts, and rambling into something that looked like an actual book. She pushed me to think a little deeper, to provide more concrete examples, and not to make statements that, while they would make a good tweet, were not supported by facts and/or data. Sarah adopted my book baby as if it was her very own, pouring an incredible amount of time and energy into making it better. Thanks for caring as much as me about these ideas, Sarah. You and Rodney taking my late night calls and early morning texts was invaluable to me as a writer . . . and as a human. Love you both and looking forward to more manhattan nights at your place!

Dan Scott made this book better by calling me out. Dan is one of my best friends in the world, which meant he had permission to blast straight through my enneagram three facade and bravado, call me out on my redundant padding of content, my grandstanding, and ultimately drag me kicking and screaming to a final manuscript that was far more helpful for you to read, and less egotistical (believe it or not). You're a good man Dan, and a great mate. Thanks for making me better.

To the team at Orange who gave me the space and confidence to write this book. Your belief in me, your creativity, your friendship, and the way you continue to cheer for me and my family is appreciated more than words can express. Special shout out to Brian and Mike for working closely on this project, Reggie and Kristen for your confidence, and Ashley Bohinc, for inspiring me to start this process and constantly texting me to check in on how it was going.

Some close friends read through excerpts of this book in the early stages, gave their feedback on titles and covers, sorted my ideas out on Zoom calls, and generally supported me with their encouragement and wisdom. So a special thanks goes to Kacey Lanier, Stuart Hall, Kenny Jahng, Van Baird, Will Vest, Clark Campbell, Beau Coffron, Jonathan Gullo, Caz and Murray Holmes, Duncan Banks, Laurie Bulson, and Katie Allred. You all are legends.

To church innovation leaders like Bobby Gruenewald, Carey Nieuwhof, Nona Jones, Jonathan Pokluda, Frank Blake, Bob Goff and Mark Batterson: Thanks for the inspiration, wisdom, and your passion to see the Church thrive around the world. I read everything you all write or produce. And thanks to Tim Lucas for taking a risk on hiring a TV sports reporter from Australia and moving him to New Jersey to become the 8th online pastor in the world (and for introducing me to Mischief Night; which led to me ending up in a police car).

There are also a plethora of people in the church online/church communications community who have become like family over the years. These people have supported and encouraged me as an online and social media pastor, either in-person or from afar. You have all challenged my thinking, inspired my ideas, and many of you have become close friends. A lot of these people feature in the final chapter of this book (if you don't read anything else in this book, read the last chapter . . . it's my favorite chapter) where they share their thoughts

ACKNOWLEDGEMENTS

and predictions about the future of the Church. You all need to write books as well to share your wisdom with the world!

I also want to acknowledge the staff and leadership at North Point Ministries in Atlanta, who allowed me to experiment, test, fail, prototype, pretotype, and most of all, learn. Special thanks to the North Point Creative Services team for your hard work and dedication to making and distributing content, and taking the weird out of church.

I especially want to thank Andy Stanley. His name appears many times in this book because his friendship and encouragement allowed me to learn about what Church is, and dream about what it could be. From the moment we met during the making of the *Christmas in Bevelton* video, you were someone I looked up to and am inspired by. Yours and Sandra's friendship means the world to me. We love you both.

And finally, to Paul Rudd . . . because I think we'd be best mates, but he's not even on social media, so I know he'll never read this. Unless someone tells him.

Thanks everyone. I love your work!

CONNECT EVERY PARENT TO YOUR CHURCH WITH ONE SIMPLE APP

There has never been a more important time to re-engage families everywhere.

Start customizing the Parent Cue app today!

PARENTCUEAPP.CHURCH